50 Canadian Lunch Recipes for Home

By: Kelly Johnson

Table of Contents

- Maple Glazed Salmon
- Poutine
- Butter Tarts
- Nanaimo Bars
- Tourtière
- Lobster Rolls
- Montreal Bagels
- Wild Mushroom Soup
- Smoked Salmon Eggs Benedict
- Peameal Bacon Sandwich
- Quebec-style Meat Pie
- Bannock
- Acadian Chicken Fricot
- Saskatoon Berry Pie
- BeaverTails
- Ketchup Chips Crusted Chicken
- Blueberry Grunt
- Newfoundland Jigg's Dinner
- Fiddlehead Salad
- Chicken Pot Pie
- Maritime Seafood Chowder
- Alberta Beef Stew
- Nova Scotia Hodge Podge
- Ontario Apple Crisp
- Quebec Sugar Pie (Tarte au Sucre)
- Wild Rice and Mushroom Pilaf
- Bison Burgers
- Prairie Perogies
- Calgary Ginger Beef
- Atlantic Cod Cakes
- Ontario Corn Chowder
- Manitoba Cabbage Rolls
- Quebecois Tourtière
- Wild Blueberry Pancakes
- B.C. Spot Prawns

- Alberta Bison Chili
- Maple Butter Tart Cheesecake
- Maritime Fish Cakes
- Quebec Maple Sugar Pie
- Canadian Club Caesar Cocktail
- Ontario Butter Tart Cake
- Saskatchewan Lentil Soup
- Nunavut Caribou Stew
- New Brunswick Chicken Fricot
- Prince Edward Island Mussel Chowder
- Yukon Bison Stew
- Northern Ontario Pickerel Fillets
- Ontario Cherry Clafoutis
- Quebecois Pouding Chômeur (Poor Man's Pudding)
- Canadian Rocky Road Ice Cream

Maple Glazed Salmon

Ingredients:

- 4 salmon fillets (about 6 ounces each), skin-on
- Salt and pepper, to taste
- 1/4 cup maple syrup
- 2 tablespoons soy sauce (or tamari for gluten-free)
- 1 tablespoon Dijon mustard
- 1 tablespoon olive oil
- 2 cloves garlic, minced
- 1 teaspoon grated fresh ginger (optional)
- Fresh chopped parsley or green onions, for garnish

Instructions:

1. Prepare the Glaze:
    - In a small bowl, whisk together the maple syrup, soy sauce, Dijon mustard, minced garlic, and grated ginger (if using). Set aside.
2. Prepare the Salmon:
    - Pat the salmon fillets dry with paper towels and season both sides with salt and pepper.
3. Cook the Salmon:
    - Heat the olive oil in a large skillet over medium-high heat. Place the salmon fillets in the skillet, skin-side down if they have skin.
    - Cook for 4-5 minutes, depending on thickness, until the salmon easily releases from the skillet and the skin is crispy and golden brown. Flip the fillets and cook for another 3-4 minutes, or until the salmon is cooked to your desired doneness.
4. Glaze the Salmon:
    - Reduce the heat to medium-low. Pour the maple glaze over the salmon fillets in the skillet.
    - Spoon the glaze over the salmon as it simmers and thickens, coating the fillets evenly. Cook for 1-2 minutes until the glaze has slightly caramelized and the salmon is fully cooked through.
5. Serve:
    - Remove the skillet from heat. Transfer the glazed salmon fillets to serving plates or a platter.
    - Garnish with fresh chopped parsley or green onions.
6. Enjoy:

    - Serve the maple glazed salmon hot, accompanied by your favorite side dishes such as rice, quinoa, or roasted vegetables.

This maple glazed salmon is a perfect balance of sweet and savory flavors, making it a wonderful dish for both weeknight dinners and special occasions.

Poutine

Ingredients:

- 4 large potatoes (Russet or Yukon Gold), peeled and cut into fries
- Vegetable oil, for frying
- Salt, to taste

For the Gravy:

- 2 tablespoons unsalted butter
- 2 tablespoons all-purpose flour
- 2 cups beef broth (or chicken broth for a lighter version)
- Salt and pepper, to taste

For Assembly:

- 2 cups cheese curds (preferably fresh, but you can also use mozzarella cheese if curds are not available)

Instructions:

1. Prepare the Fries:
    - Cut the peeled potatoes into fries, about 1/4 inch thick. Rinse them in cold water to remove excess starch, then pat dry with paper towels.
    - Heat vegetable oil in a deep fryer or large pot to 325°F (165°C). Fry the potatoes in batches until light golden and just starting to cook through, about 3-4 minutes per batch. Remove from oil and drain on paper towels. Let them cool slightly.
2. Prepare the Gravy:
    - In a medium saucepan, melt the butter over medium heat. Add the flour and whisk constantly for 1-2 minutes to make a roux.
    - Gradually pour in the beef broth, whisking continuously to avoid lumps. Bring the gravy to a simmer and cook until thickened, about 5-7 minutes. Season with salt and pepper to taste. Keep warm over low heat.
3. Fry the Fries Again:
    - Increase the oil temperature to 375°F (190°C). Fry the par-cooked fries in batches again until crispy and golden brown, about 2-3 minutes per batch. Drain on paper towels and immediately sprinkle with salt while hot.
4. Assemble the Poutine:
    - Arrange a portion of hot fries on a serving plate or in a shallow bowl.

- Sprinkle a generous amount of cheese curds over the fries while they are still hot, allowing them to slightly melt.
- Ladle hot gravy over the fries and cheese curds, ensuring all parts are covered with gravy. The heat will further melt the cheese curds.
5. Serve Immediately:
    - Enjoy the poutine immediately while the fries are crispy and the cheese curds are melty. Poutine is best served hot and fresh.

Poutine is a comforting and indulgent dish that can be customized with various toppings like pulled pork, bacon, or vegetables, but the classic version with cheese curds and gravy remains a Canadian favorite.

Butter Tarts

Ingredients:

For the Pastry:

- 1 1/4 cups all-purpose flour
- 1/4 teaspoon salt
- 1/2 cup unsalted butter, cold and cut into small cubes
- 2-3 tablespoons ice water

For the Filling:

- 1/2 cup packed brown sugar
- 1/2 cup corn syrup (light or dark)
- 1/4 cup unsalted butter, melted
- 1 large egg, lightly beaten
- 1 teaspoon vanilla extract
- 1/4 teaspoon salt
- Optional: 1/2 cup raisins, chopped nuts, or both

Instructions:

1. Prepare the Pastry:
    - In a mixing bowl, whisk together the flour and salt.
    - Add the cold cubed butter and use a pastry cutter or your fingers to work the butter into the flour until the mixture resembles coarse crumbs.
    - Gradually add the ice water, 1 tablespoon at a time, mixing with a fork until the dough just begins to come together. It should hold together when pinched.
2. Form the Dough:
    - Gather the dough into a ball, flatten into a disc, wrap in plastic wrap, and refrigerate for at least 30 minutes.
3. Preheat the Oven:
    - Preheat your oven to 375°F (190°C). Lightly grease a 12-cup muffin tin or use butter tart pans.
4. Make the Filling:
    - In a bowl, whisk together the brown sugar, corn syrup, melted butter, beaten egg, vanilla extract, and salt until smooth.
    - If using, stir in the optional raisins or chopped nuts.
5. Roll Out the Pastry:

- On a lightly floured surface, roll out the chilled pastry dough to about 1/8 inch thick. Use a round cutter or a glass slightly larger than the muffin tin cups to cut out circles of dough.
6. Assemble the Tarts:
   - Gently press each circle of dough into the muffin tin cups or butter tart pans, forming small pastry shells.
   - Fill each pastry shell about 2/3 full with the prepared filling mixture.
7. Bake:
   - Bake the butter tarts in the preheated oven for 15-18 minutes, or until the pastry is golden and the filling is set but still slightly jiggly in the center.
8. Cool and Serve:
   - Remove the butter tarts from the oven and let them cool in the pan for a few minutes.
   - Carefully transfer the tarts to a wire rack to cool completely before serving.
9. Enjoy:
   - Serve the butter tarts at room temperature. They can be enjoyed plain or with a dollop of whipped cream or vanilla ice cream.

Butter tarts are a delightful treat that captures the essence of Canadian baking traditions. They are perfect for special occasions or anytime you crave a sweet, gooey pastry.

Nanaimo Bars

Ingredients:

For the Base:

- 1/2 cup unsalted butter, melted
- 1/4 cup granulated sugar
- 1/3 cup unsweetened cocoa powder
- 1 large egg, beaten
- 1 teaspoon vanilla extract
- 2 cups graham cracker crumbs
- 1 cup sweetened shredded coconut
- 1/2 cup chopped walnuts or pecans (optional)

For the Middle Layer:

- 1/2 cup unsalted butter, softened
- 2 cups powdered sugar (icing sugar)
- 2 tablespoons custard powder (or vanilla pudding mix)
- 2-3 tablespoons milk or cream

For the Top Layer:

- 4 ounces semi-sweet or dark chocolate, chopped
- 2 tablespoons unsalted butter

Instructions:

1. Prepare the Base:
    - In a medium bowl, combine the melted butter, granulated sugar, cocoa powder, beaten egg, and vanilla extract.
    - Stir in the graham cracker crumbs, shredded coconut, and chopped nuts (if using), until well combined and the mixture resembles a thick, moist dough.
2. Press into Pan:
    - Press the mixture firmly and evenly into the bottom of an ungreased 9x9-inch square baking pan. Use the back of a spoon or your hands to smooth it out.
3. Chill:
    - Place the pan in the refrigerator while you prepare the middle layer.

4. Make the Middle Layer:
    - In a mixing bowl, beat together the softened butter, powdered sugar, and custard powder (or vanilla pudding mix) until smooth and creamy.
    - Add milk or cream, 1 tablespoon at a time, until the mixture is spreadable but still thick.
5. Spread Over Base:
    - Remove the pan from the refrigerator and spread the middle layer evenly over the chilled base layer. Use a spatula to smooth the top.
6. Chill Again:
    - Return the pan to the refrigerator and chill for at least 30 minutes, or until the middle layer is firm.
7. Prepare the Top Layer:
    - In a microwave-safe bowl or over a double boiler, melt the chopped chocolate and butter together until smooth, stirring frequently.
    - Pour the melted chocolate mixture over the chilled middle layer, spreading it evenly with a spatula.
8. Chill Until Set:
    - Return the pan to the refrigerator and chill the Nanaimo bars for at least 1-2 hours, or until the chocolate topping is firm.
9. Cut and Serve:
    - Once fully chilled and set, use a sharp knife to cut the Nanaimo bars into squares.
    - Serve the bars chilled. They can be stored in an airtight container in the refrigerator for up to one week.

Nanaimo bars are a decadent and delicious treat that's perfect for special occasions or anytime you crave a sweet and creamy dessert. Enjoy this iconic Canadian delicacy with friends and family!

Tourtière

Ingredients:

For the Pastry:

- 2 1/2 cups all-purpose flour
- 1/2 teaspoon salt
- 1 cup unsalted butter, cold and cut into cubes
- 1/2 cup ice water

For the Filling:

- 1 lb ground pork
- 1/2 lb ground veal or beef (or a combination with pork)
- 1 small onion, finely chopped
- 2 cloves garlic, minced
- 1/2 teaspoon ground cinnamon
- 1/4 teaspoon ground cloves
- 1/4 teaspoon ground nutmeg
- Salt and pepper, to taste
- 1 cup beef or chicken broth
- 1/2 cup breadcrumbs
- 1 tablespoon chopped fresh parsley (optional)
- 1 egg, beaten (for egg wash)

Instructions:

1. Make the Pastry:
    - In a large mixing bowl, whisk together the flour and salt. Add the cold cubed butter and use a pastry cutter or your fingers to work the butter into the flour until the mixture resembles coarse crumbs.
    - Gradually add the ice water, 1 tablespoon at a time, mixing with a fork until the dough just begins to come together. It should hold together when pinched.
    - Gather the dough into a ball, divide it in half, flatten into two discs, wrap each in plastic wrap, and refrigerate for at least 30 minutes.
2. Prepare the Filling:
    - In a large skillet or frying pan, cook the ground pork and veal (or beef) over medium-high heat until browned and cooked through, breaking up the meat with a spoon as it cooks.

- Add the finely chopped onion, minced garlic, ground cinnamon, ground cloves, ground nutmeg, salt, and pepper. Cook for another 3-4 minutes until the onion is softened and fragrant.
- Stir in the beef or chicken broth and bring to a simmer. Reduce the heat to low and simmer gently for 10-15 minutes, stirring occasionally, until most of the liquid has evaporated.
- Remove from heat and stir in the breadcrumbs and chopped parsley (if using). Let the filling cool completely.

3. Assemble the Tourtière:
    - Preheat your oven to 375°F (190°C). Lightly grease a 9-inch pie dish.
    - On a lightly floured surface, roll out one disc of chilled pastry dough into a circle large enough to line the bottom and sides of the pie dish. Gently press the dough into the dish, leaving any excess hanging over the edges.
    - Spoon the cooled meat filling evenly into the pastry-lined dish, pressing down gently to compact it.

4. Add the Top Crust:
    - Roll out the second disc of chilled pastry dough into a circle large enough to cover the pie dish. Place it over the filling.
    - Trim the excess dough, leaving about a 1-inch overhang. Fold the overhang under the bottom crust edge, pressing together to seal. Crimp the edges with a fork or pinch with your fingers to create a decorative border.

5. Bake:
    - Brush the top of the pie with the beaten egg to create a shiny finish.
    - Cut a few small slits in the top crust to allow steam to escape during baking.
    - Place the tourtière on a baking sheet (to catch any drips) and bake in the preheated oven for 45-50 minutes, or until the crust is golden brown.

6. Serve:
    - Remove the tourtière from the oven and let it cool for at least 10-15 minutes before slicing and serving.

Tourtière is often served with a side of ketchup or cranberry sauce. It's a comforting and flavorful dish that's perfect for holiday gatherings or any special occasion. Enjoy this taste of Quebecois tradition!

Lobster Rolls

Ingredients:

- 4 lobster tails (about 6-8 ounces each), cooked and meat removed
- 1/4 cup mayonnaise
- 1 tablespoon lemon juice
- 1 celery stalk, finely chopped
- 2 tablespoons chopped fresh chives or green onions
- Salt and pepper, to taste
- 4 soft hot dog buns or New England-style split-top rolls
- 2 tablespoons unsalted butter, melted
- Optional: lettuce leaves or shredded lettuce for serving

Instructions:

1. Prepare the Lobster Meat:
    - Cook the lobster tails according to your preferred method (boiling, steaming, or grilling) until the meat is cooked through and tender. Let them cool slightly.
    - Remove the lobster meat from the shells and chop it into bite-sized chunks. Set aside.
2. Make the Lobster Salad:
    - In a bowl, combine the mayonnaise, lemon juice, chopped celery, and chopped chives or green onions. Mix well.
    - Add the chopped lobster meat to the bowl and gently toss to coat the lobster with the dressing.
    - Season with salt and pepper to taste. Adjust the seasoning as needed.
3. Prepare the Rolls:
    - Heat a large skillet or griddle over medium heat. Brush the outsides of the hot dog buns or split-top rolls with melted butter.
    - Toast the buns on the skillet until golden brown and crisp on both sides, about 1-2 minutes per side. Remove from heat.
4. Assemble the Lobster Rolls:
    - If using, place a lettuce leaf or shredded lettuce inside each toasted bun for added crunch.
    - Divide the lobster salad evenly among the toasted buns, spooning it into the center of each bun.
5. Serve:

- Serve the lobster rolls immediately, while the buns are still warm and the lobster salad is chilled.
- Enjoy the lobster rolls as is or with additional lemon wedges and a side of potato chips or coleslaw.

Lobster rolls are a delightful summer treat that highlight the fresh and delicate flavor of lobster. They're perfect for outdoor picnics, beach outings, or any time you want to savor a taste of the East Coast.

Montreal Bagels

Ingredients:

For the Dough:

- 1 1/2 cups warm water (110-115°F)
- 1/4 cup granulated sugar
- 2 tablespoons active dry yeast
- 4 cups bread flour (plus extra for kneading)
- 1 1/2 teaspoons salt
- 1 tablespoon vegetable oil (for dough)
- 1/4 cup honey (for boiling)

Optional Toppings:

- Poppy seeds
- Sesame seeds

Instructions:

1. Prepare the Dough:
    - In a large mixing bowl, combine the warm water, sugar, and active dry yeast. Let it sit for 5-10 minutes until foamy.
    - Add the bread flour and salt to the yeast mixture. Stir until a dough forms.
    - Transfer the dough to a lightly floured surface and knead for about 8-10 minutes, adding more flour as needed, until the dough is smooth and elastic.
    - Shape the dough into a ball and place it in a lightly oiled bowl, turning to coat. Cover with a clean kitchen towel and let it rise in a warm, draft-free place for 1-2 hours, or until doubled in size.
2. Shape the Bagels:
    - Punch down the risen dough and divide it into 12 equal portions. Roll each portion into a smooth ball.
    - Flatten each ball slightly and use your fingers to poke a hole through the center. Stretch and shape the dough into a ring, ensuring the hole in the center is about 1-2 inches in diameter.
3. Boil the Bagels:
    - Preheat your oven to 450°F (230°C). Line a baking sheet with parchment paper and lightly grease it.

        - In a large pot, bring water and honey to a boil. Reduce the heat to maintain a gentle simmer.
        - Boil the bagels, 3-4 at a time (depending on the size of your pot), for 1-2 minutes per side. Use a slotted spoon to flip them halfway through. Remove them from the water and drain briefly on a clean kitchen towel.
4. Add Toppings (Optional):
        - While the bagels are still wet, sprinkle them with poppy seeds, sesame seeds, or any other toppings of your choice. Press the toppings lightly into the dough.
5. Bake the Bagels:
        - Place the boiled and topped bagels on the prepared baking sheet.
        - Bake in the preheated oven for 15-20 minutes, or until the bagels are golden brown and cooked through. Rotate the baking sheet halfway through baking for even browning.
6. Cool and Serve:
        - Transfer the baked bagels to a wire rack to cool completely before serving.

Montreal bagels are best enjoyed fresh and warm, sliced and served with cream cheese, smoked salmon, or your favorite toppings. They are a delightful twist on the classic bagel, offering a chewy texture and subtly sweet flavor that's uniquely Montreal.

Wild Mushroom Soup

Ingredients:

- 1 lb mixed wild mushrooms (such as cremini, shiitake, oyster, chanterelle, porcini), cleaned and sliced
- 4 tablespoons unsalted butter
- 1 large onion, diced
- 2 cloves garlic, minced
- 1 teaspoon fresh thyme leaves (or 1/2 teaspoon dried thyme)
- 4 cups vegetable or chicken broth
- 1 cup heavy cream (or substitute with half-and-half for a lighter version)
- Salt and pepper, to taste
- Chopped fresh parsley or chives, for garnish
- Crusty bread, for serving (optional)

Instructions:

1. Sauté the Mushrooms:
   - In a large pot or Dutch oven, melt 2 tablespoons of butter over medium heat.
   - Add the sliced mushrooms and cook, stirring occasionally, until they are softened and lightly browned, about 8-10 minutes. Remove half of the mushrooms and set aside for garnish.
2. Cook the Aromatics:
   - In the same pot, add the remaining 2 tablespoons of butter. Add the diced onion and cook until softened and translucent, about 5-7 minutes.
   - Stir in the minced garlic and thyme leaves, and cook for another 1-2 minutes until fragrant.
3. Simmer the Soup:
   - Return the reserved sautéed mushrooms to the pot. Pour in the vegetable or chicken broth, stirring to combine.
   - Bring the soup to a boil, then reduce the heat to low and let it simmer for 15-20 minutes to allow the flavors to meld together.
4. Blend the Soup:
   - Using an immersion blender, blend the soup until smooth and creamy. Alternatively, carefully transfer the soup in batches to a blender and blend until smooth, then return to the pot.
5. Add Cream and Season:

- Stir in the heavy cream (or half-and-half) and season with salt and pepper to taste. Adjust seasoning as needed.
6. Serve:
    - Ladle the wild mushroom soup into bowls. Garnish each serving with the reserved sautéed mushrooms and chopped fresh parsley or chives.
    - Serve the soup hot, optionally with crusty bread on the side for dipping.

Enjoy this comforting wild mushroom soup as a starter or a light main course. It's packed with earthy flavors and makes a perfect dish for mushroom lovers and anyone seeking a cozy meal.

Smoked Salmon Eggs Benedict

Ingredients:

For the Hollandaise Sauce:

- 3 large egg yolks
- 1 tablespoon lemon juice
- 1/2 cup unsalted butter, melted
- Salt and cayenne pepper, to taste

For the Eggs Benedict:

- 4 English muffins, split and toasted
- 8 slices smoked salmon
- 4 large eggs
- 1 tablespoon white vinegar
- Fresh dill or chives, chopped (for garnish)
- Salt and pepper, to taste

Instructions:

1. Prepare the Hollandaise Sauce:
    - Fill a saucepan with 1-2 inches of water and bring it to a simmer over medium heat.
    - In a heatproof bowl that fits snugly over the saucepan (but does not touch the water), whisk together the egg yolks and lemon juice until smooth.
    - Place the bowl over the simmering water (double boiler method) and whisk constantly until the mixture thickens slightly, about 2-3 minutes.
    - Gradually drizzle in the melted butter, whisking constantly, until the hollandaise sauce is smooth and creamy.
    - Season with salt and a pinch of cayenne pepper, adjusting to taste. Keep the sauce warm over the warm water bath, stirring occasionally.
2. Poach the Eggs:
    - Fill a large saucepan with water and add the white vinegar. Bring the water to a gentle simmer over medium heat.
    - Crack each egg into a small bowl or cup. Create a gentle whirlpool in the simmering water using a spoon.
    - Carefully slide each egg into the center of the whirlpool. Poach the eggs for about 3-4 minutes, until the whites are set and the yolks are still runny.

- Remove the poached eggs with a slotted spoon and drain them on a plate lined with paper towels.
3. Assemble the Eggs Benedict:
    - Place toasted English muffin halves on serving plates.
    - Top each half with a slice of smoked salmon.
    - Carefully place a poached egg on top of each salmon slice.
4. Finish and Serve:
    - Spoon hollandaise sauce generously over each poached egg.
    - Garnish with chopped fresh dill or chives, and season with salt and pepper to taste.
    - Serve the smoked salmon eggs Benedict immediately, accompanied by a side of fresh fruit or salad.

Smoked salmon eggs Benedict is a delightful and elegant dish, perfect for brunch or a special occasion. The creamy hollandaise sauce complements the smoky richness of the salmon and the perfectly poached eggs. Enjoy this restaurant-style breakfast at home!

Peameal Bacon Sandwich

Ingredients:

- 4 slices peameal bacon (about 1/4 inch thick)
- 4 sandwich buns or rolls (such as Kaiser rolls or English muffins)
- Butter or vegetable oil, for cooking
- Optional toppings: lettuce, tomato slices, cheese (cheddar or Swiss), mustard, mayonnaise

Instructions:

1. Cook the Peameal Bacon:
    - Heat a large skillet or frying pan over medium-high heat. Add a small amount of butter or vegetable oil to coat the bottom of the skillet.
    - Place the peameal bacon slices in the skillet and cook for about 3-4 minutes per side, or until golden brown and cooked through. The bacon should be crispy on the outside and tender inside.
2. Prepare the Sandwich Buns:
    - While the bacon is cooking, lightly toast the sandwich buns or rolls under a broiler or in a toaster oven until they are golden brown.
3. Assemble the Sandwiches:
    - Spread butter or your preferred condiment (mustard, mayonnaise) on the toasted buns, if desired.
    - Place a cooked peameal bacon slice on each bottom half of the sandwich buns.
    - Add any additional toppings you like, such as lettuce, tomato slices, or cheese.
4. Serve:
    - Place the top halves of the sandwich buns over the toppings to form sandwiches.
    - Serve the peameal bacon sandwiches immediately, while the bacon is still warm and crispy.

Peameal bacon sandwiches are perfect for a quick and satisfying breakfast, brunch, or lunch option. They showcase the savory flavor and unique texture of peameal bacon, paired with your favorite toppings on a soft bun. Enjoy this Canadian classic at home!

Quebec-style Meat Pie

Ingredients:

For the Pastry:

- 2 1/2 cups all-purpose flour
- 1/2 teaspoon salt
- 1 cup unsalted butter, cold and cut into cubes
- 1/2 cup ice water

For the Filling:

- 1 lb ground pork
- 1/2 lb ground beef
- 1 small onion, finely chopped
- 2 cloves garlic, minced
- 1/2 teaspoon ground cinnamon
- 1/4 teaspoon ground cloves
- 1/4 teaspoon ground nutmeg
- 1/4 teaspoon ground allspice
- Salt and pepper, to taste
- 1/2 cup beef or chicken broth
- 1/2 cup mashed potatoes (optional, for texture and binding)
- 1 egg, beaten (for egg wash)

Instructions:

1. Make the Pastry:
    - In a large mixing bowl, whisk together the flour and salt.
    - Add the cold cubed butter and use a pastry cutter or your fingers to work the butter into the flour until the mixture resembles coarse crumbs.
    - Gradually add the ice water, 1 tablespoon at a time, mixing with a fork until the dough just begins to come together. It should hold together when pinched.
    - Gather the dough into a ball, divide it in half, flatten into two discs, wrap each in plastic wrap, and refrigerate for at least 30 minutes.
2. Prepare the Filling:
    - In a large skillet or frying pan, cook the ground pork and beef over medium-high heat until browned and cooked through, breaking up the meat with a spoon as it cooks.

- Add the finely chopped onion and minced garlic. Cook for another 3-4 minutes until the onion is softened and translucent.
            - Stir in the ground cinnamon, ground cloves, ground nutmeg, ground allspice, salt, and pepper. Cook for another minute until fragrant.
            - Add the beef or chicken broth and mashed potatoes (if using), stirring to combine. Bring to a simmer and cook for 5-7 minutes, stirring occasionally, until most of the liquid has evaporated.
            - Remove from heat and let the filling cool completely.
    3. Assemble the Tourtière:
            - Preheat your oven to 400°F (200°C). Lightly grease a 9-inch pie dish.
            - On a lightly floured surface, roll out one disc of chilled pastry dough into a circle large enough to line the bottom and sides of the pie dish. Gently press the dough into the dish, leaving any excess hanging over the edges.
            - Spoon the cooled meat filling evenly into the pastry-lined dish, pressing down gently to compact it.
    4. Add the Top Crust:
            - Roll out the second disc of chilled pastry dough into a circle large enough to cover the pie dish. Place it over the filling.
            - Trim the excess dough, leaving about a 1-inch overhang. Fold the overhang under the bottom crust edge, pressing together to seal. Crimp the edges with a fork or pinch with your fingers to create a decorative border.
            - Cut a few small slits in the top crust to allow steam to escape during baking.
    5. Bake:
            - Brush the top of the pie with the beaten egg to create a shiny finish.
            - Place the tourtière on a baking sheet (to catch any drips) and bake in the preheated oven for 45-50 minutes, or until the crust is golden brown and the filling is heated through.
    6. Cool and Serve:
            - Remove the tourtière from the oven and let it cool for at least 10-15 minutes before slicing and serving.

Tourtière is traditionally served warm, often with a side of ketchup or cranberry sauce. It's a comforting and flavorful dish that's perfect for holiday gatherings or any special occasion, showcasing the hearty flavors of Quebecois cuisine.

Bannock

Ingredients:

- 2 cups all-purpose flour
- 2 teaspoons baking powder
- 1/2 teaspoon salt
- 1/2 cup cold water (approximately)
- Vegetable oil or butter, for frying

Instructions:

1. Mix Dry Ingredients:
   - In a large bowl, whisk together the all-purpose flour, baking powder, and salt until well combined.
2. Form Dough:
   - Gradually add the cold water to the dry ingredients, mixing with a spoon or your hands until a soft dough forms. You may not need all of the water, so add it gradually until the dough comes together and isn't too sticky.
3. Knead the Dough:
   - Turn the dough out onto a lightly floured surface and knead it gently for a few minutes until smooth. Avoid overworking the dough, as bannock should be tender.
4. Shape and Cook:
   - Divide the dough into portions, depending on how big you want your bannock. You can shape it into rounds, ovals, or flatten it into disks.
5. Heat Oil or Butter:
   - In a large skillet or frying pan, heat a generous amount of vegetable oil or butter over medium heat. You want enough oil to cover the bottom of the pan.
6. Fry the Bannock:
   - Carefully place the shaped dough into the hot oil or butter. Cook for about 3-4 minutes on each side, or until golden brown and cooked through. Adjust the heat as needed to prevent burning.
7. Serve:
   - Remove the cooked bannock from the pan and drain on paper towels to remove excess oil.
   - Serve the bannock warm, either plain or with toppings like butter, honey, jam, or as a side to soups and stews.

Bannock is a simple yet delicious bread that can be enjoyed in various ways. It's a staple in Indigenous cuisine and has become popular across Canada, often enjoyed during outdoor activities like camping or as a comforting side dish.

Acadian Chicken Fricot

Ingredients:

- 1 whole chicken (about 3-4 lbs), cut into pieces (or use bone-in chicken thighs and drumsticks)
- 2 tablespoons butter or vegetable oil
- 1 large onion, chopped
- 2-3 garlic cloves, minced
- 4 cups chicken broth
- 4 cups water
- 4 medium potatoes, peeled and diced
- 2 carrots, peeled and diced (optional)
- 1 celery stalk, diced (optional)
- 1 bay leaf
- Salt and pepper, to taste
- Chopped fresh parsley, for garnish (optional)

Instructions:

1. Brown the Chicken:
   - In a large pot or Dutch oven, heat the butter or vegetable oil over medium-high heat.
   - Add the chicken pieces and brown them on all sides, about 3-4 minutes per side. Remove the chicken from the pot and set aside.
2. Sauté the Aromatics:
   - In the same pot, add the chopped onion and garlic. Sauté for 3-4 minutes, until softened and fragrant.
3. Simmer the Stew:
   - Return the browned chicken pieces to the pot.
   - Pour in the chicken broth and water, stirring to combine.
   - Add the diced potatoes, carrots (if using), celery (if using), and bay leaf to the pot.
   - Season with salt and pepper to taste.
   - Bring the mixture to a boil, then reduce the heat to low. Cover and simmer for about 30-40 minutes, or until the chicken is cooked through and the vegetables are tender.
4. Finish and Serve:
   - Remove the bay leaf from the stew.
   - Taste and adjust seasoning if needed.

- Serve hot, garnished with chopped fresh parsley if desired.

Acadian Chicken Fricot is a comforting and wholesome dish, perfect for cold winter days or any time you crave a hearty meal. It's often served with fresh bread or biscuits on the side. Enjoy this taste of Acadian cuisine from the Maritime provinces of Canada!

Saskatoon Berry Pie

Ingredients:

For the Pie Crust:

- 2 1/2 cups all-purpose flour
- 1 teaspoon salt
- 1 cup unsalted butter, cold and cut into cubes
- 6-8 tablespoons ice water

For the Filling:

- 5 cups Saskatoon berries, fresh or frozen
- 1 cup granulated sugar
- 1/4 cup all-purpose flour
- 1 tablespoon lemon juice
- 1/2 teaspoon ground cinnamon (optional)
- 1 tablespoon unsalted butter, cut into small pieces

For Assembly:

- 1 egg, beaten (for egg wash)
- Granulated sugar, for sprinkling

Instructions:

1. Make the Pie Crust:
    - In a large bowl, whisk together the flour and salt.
    - Add the cold cubed butter to the flour mixture. Using a pastry cutter or your fingers, work the butter into the flour until the mixture resembles coarse crumbs.
    - Gradually add the ice water, 1 tablespoon at a time, mixing with a fork, until the dough just holds together when pinched. You may not need to use all of the water.
    - Divide the dough in half, shape each half into a disk, wrap them in plastic wrap, and refrigerate for at least 1 hour.
2. Prepare the Filling:
    - In a large bowl, combine the Saskatoon berries, granulated sugar, flour, lemon juice, and ground cinnamon (if using). Gently toss until the berries are coated evenly.

3. **Assemble the Pie:**
    - Preheat your oven to 400°F (200°C).
    - On a lightly floured surface, roll out one disk of chilled pie dough into a circle large enough to line a 9-inch pie dish. Carefully transfer the dough to the pie dish, gently pressing it into the bottom and sides.
    - Spoon the Saskatoon berry filling into the prepared pie crust, spreading it evenly.
    - Dot the filling with pieces of unsalted butter.
4. **Top the Pie:**
    - Roll out the second disk of chilled pie dough into a circle large enough to cover the pie. You can either place the dough over the filling whole, or cut it into strips for a lattice crust.
    - Trim any excess dough hanging over the edges of the pie dish. Press the edges of the top and bottom crusts together, then fold under and crimp as desired.
5. **Bake the Pie:**
    - Brush the top of the pie crust with the beaten egg and sprinkle with granulated sugar for a shiny, golden finish.
    - Place the pie on a baking sheet (to catch any drips) and bake in the preheated oven for 45-50 minutes, or until the crust is golden brown and the filling is bubbly.
6. **Cool and Serve:**
    - Allow the Saskatoon berry pie to cool on a wire rack for at least 1 hour before serving to allow the filling to set.
    - Serve slices of pie warm or at room temperature, optionally with a scoop of vanilla ice cream or a dollop of whipped cream.

Saskatoon berry pie is a delightful dessert that celebrates the unique flavor of these Canadian berries. Enjoy this homemade pie with family and friends, especially during the summer months when Saskatoon berries are in season!

BeaverTails

Ingredients:

For the Dough:

- 1 cup warm water (about 110°F)
- 1 tablespoon granulated sugar
- 1 package (2 1/4 teaspoons) active dry yeast
- 3 cups all-purpose flour
- 1/2 teaspoon salt
- 1/4 cup unsalted butter, melted
- Vegetable oil, for frying

For Topping:

- 1/2 cup granulated sugar
- 1 teaspoon ground cinnamon
- Optional toppings: Nutella, chocolate sauce, caramel sauce, whipped cream, berries, etc.

Instructions:

1. Prepare the Dough:
   - In a small bowl, combine the warm water, sugar, and yeast. Let it sit for 5-10 minutes until foamy.
   - In a large mixing bowl, whisk together the flour and salt. Add the melted butter and activated yeast mixture.
   - Mix until a soft dough forms. Turn the dough out onto a lightly floured surface and knead for about 5-7 minutes, or until smooth and elastic.
   - Place the dough in a greased bowl, cover with a clean kitchen towel, and let it rise in a warm place for about 1 hour, or until doubled in size.
2. Shape and Fry the BeaverTails:
   - Punch down the risen dough and divide it into 8 equal portions. Shape each portion into an oval or rectangle shape resembling a beaver's tail.
   - In a large skillet or deep fryer, heat vegetable oil to 350°F (175°C).
   - Carefully place one piece of dough into the hot oil and fry for about 2-3 minutes per side, or until golden brown and cooked through. Fry in batches, if necessary, to avoid overcrowding the pan.
   - Remove the fried BeaverTails from the oil using a slotted spoon and drain on paper towels to remove excess oil.

3. Prepare the Toppings:
    - In a shallow bowl, mix together the granulated sugar and ground cinnamon.
    - While the BeaverTails are still warm, generously coat each one in the cinnamon sugar mixture, ensuring all sides are covered.
4. Serve:
    - Serve the BeaverTails warm, optionally topped with Nutella, chocolate sauce, caramel sauce, whipped cream, berries, or your favorite toppings.

BeaverTails are best enjoyed fresh and warm, making them a popular treat at festivals, fairs, and outdoor events across Canada. This homemade version allows you to recreate this iconic Canadian snack in your own kitchen, bringing the delicious taste of BeaverTails to your home!

Ketchup Chips Crusted Chicken

Ingredients:

- 4 boneless, skinless chicken breasts
- 1 cup ketchup chips, finely crushed (about 1 small bag)
- 1/2 cup all-purpose flour
- 2 large eggs, beaten
- Salt and pepper, to taste
- Cooking oil or cooking spray

Instructions:

1. Preheat the Oven:
   - Preheat your oven to 400°F (200°C). Line a baking sheet with parchment paper or foil and lightly grease it with cooking oil or spray.
2. Prepare the Chicken:
   - Season the chicken breasts with salt and pepper on both sides.
3. Set Up Breading Station:
   - Prepare three shallow bowls or plates. Place the flour in one bowl, the beaten eggs in another, and the crushed ketchup chips in the third bowl.
4. Coat the Chicken:
   - Dredge each chicken breast in the flour, shaking off any excess.
   - Dip the floured chicken breasts into the beaten eggs, coating them thoroughly.
   - Press the chicken breasts into the crushed ketchup chips, making sure the chips adhere to both sides of the chicken.
5. Bake the Chicken:
   - Place the coated chicken breasts on the prepared baking sheet.
   - Bake in the preheated oven for 20-25 minutes, or until the chicken is cooked through and the crust is golden brown and crispy.
6. Serve:
   - Remove the ketchup chips crusted chicken from the oven and let it rest for a few minutes before serving.
   - Serve hot, garnished with fresh herbs if desired, alongside your favorite side dishes like roasted vegetables, salad, or potatoes.

Enjoy the unique and delicious flavor of ketchup chips crusted chicken, which combines the classic crunch of potato chips with tender, juicy chicken. It's a fun twist on a traditional chicken dinner that's sure to delight both kids and adults alike!

Blueberry Grunt

Ingredients:

For the Blueberry Filling:

- 4 cups fresh or frozen blueberries
- 1/2 cup granulated sugar
- 1/4 cup water
- 1 tablespoon lemon juice
- 1/2 teaspoon ground cinnamon (optional)

For the Dumplings:

- 1 cup all-purpose flour
- 2 tablespoons granulated sugar
- 1 1/2 teaspoons baking powder
- 1/4 teaspoon salt
- 1/2 cup milk
- 2 tablespoons unsalted butter, melted

Instructions:

1. Prepare the Blueberry Filling:
    - In a large saucepan, combine the blueberries, granulated sugar, water, lemon juice, and ground cinnamon (if using).
    - Bring the mixture to a boil over medium-high heat, then reduce the heat to low and simmer for about 5-7 minutes, stirring occasionally, until the blueberries release their juices and the mixture thickens slightly. Remove from heat and set aside.
2. Make the Dumplings:
    - In a medium bowl, whisk together the flour, granulated sugar, baking powder, and salt.
    - Add the milk and melted butter to the dry ingredients, stirring until just combined. The dough will be thick and sticky.
3. Assemble and Cook the Grunt:
    - Return the blueberry filling to a simmer over medium heat.
    - Drop spoonfuls of the dumpling batter onto the simmering blueberries, making 6-8 dumplings. Leave some space between the dumplings as they will expand while cooking.

            - Cover the saucepan with a tight-fitting lid. Simmer gently for about 15 minutes, or until the dumplings are cooked through (they should be puffed and cooked in the center).
    4. Serve:
        - Spoon the warm blueberry grunt into serving bowls, making sure to include some of the sauce and dumplings in each serving.
        - Serve the blueberry grunt warm, optionally topped with a scoop of vanilla ice cream or a dollop of whipped cream.

Blueberry grunt is a comforting and delicious dessert that highlights the natural sweetness of blueberries. It's a perfect dish to enjoy during the summer when blueberries are in season, or any time you're craving a cozy dessert with a touch of Canadian heritage.

Newfoundland Jigg's Dinner

Ingredients:

- 1 lb salt beef or corned beef brisket
- 4-6 medium potatoes, peeled and left whole
- 4-6 medium carrots, peeled and left whole
- 1 small head of cabbage, cored and quartered
- 1 cup yellow split peas
- 1 onion, peeled and left whole
- 1 bay leaf
- Salt and pepper, to taste
- Mustard pickles or pickled beets, for serving (optional)

Instructions:

1. Prepare the Salt Beef:
    - If using salt beef, soak it in cold water overnight to remove excess saltiness. Change the water a few times during soaking.
2. Cook the Yellow Split Peas:
    - Rinse the yellow split peas thoroughly under cold water.
    - Place the split peas in a large saucepan and cover with water. Add the whole onion and bay leaf.
    - Bring to a boil over medium-high heat, then reduce the heat to low and simmer for about 1 hour, or until the split peas are tender and have absorbed most of the water. Stir occasionally and add more water if necessary to prevent sticking. The split peas should have a thick, pudding-like consistency.
3. Prepare the Vegetables:
    - In a large pot, place the salt beef or corned beef brisket (if not already soaked, cover with water and bring to a boil, then discard the water).
    - Add enough water to cover the beef by a few inches. Bring to a boil over high heat, then reduce the heat to medium-low and simmer for about 1 hour per pound of meat, or until the beef is tender.
4. Add the Vegetables:
    - Add the whole potatoes and carrots to the pot with the beef. Continue to simmer for about 15-20 minutes, or until the vegetables are tender.
    - Add the cabbage quarters to the pot during the last 10 minutes of cooking. Cook until the cabbage is tender but still slightly crisp.
5. Serve:

- Remove the salt beef or corned beef, potatoes, carrots, and cabbage from the pot and drain well.
- Slice the beef across the grain into thin slices.
- Serve the Jiggs' Dinner hot, with a generous spoonful of yellow split peas (pease pudding) on the side.
- Optionally, serve with mustard pickles or pickled beets for added flavor.

Jiggs' Dinner is a comforting and wholesome meal that brings together the flavors of boiled meats and vegetables, accented by the unique addition of pease pudding. It's a beloved dish in Newfoundland and Labrador, often enjoyed during special occasions and family gatherings.

Fiddlehead Salad

Ingredients:

- 1 lb fresh fiddleheads
- 2 tablespoons olive oil
- 2 tablespoons lemon juice
- 1 garlic clove, minced
- Salt and pepper, to taste
- 1/4 cup chopped fresh herbs (such as parsley, dill, or chives)
- Optional additions: cherry tomatoes, cucumber slices, radishes

Instructions:

1. Prepare the Fiddleheads:
    - Rinse the fiddleheads thoroughly under cold water to remove any dirt or debris. Trim off any brown ends or tough stems.
    - Bring a large pot of salted water to a boil. Add the fiddleheads and cook for 7-10 minutes, or until they are tender but still slightly crisp.
    - Drain the fiddleheads and immediately plunge them into a bowl of ice water to stop the cooking process and preserve their bright green color. Drain well.
2. Make the Dressing:
    - In a small bowl, whisk together the olive oil, lemon juice, minced garlic, salt, and pepper.
3. Assemble the Salad:
    - In a large bowl, combine the blanched fiddleheads with the chopped fresh herbs.
    - Pour the dressing over the fiddleheads and herbs, tossing gently to coat evenly.
    - Add any optional additions like cherry tomatoes, cucumber slices, or radishes, if desired.
4. Serve:
    - Serve the fiddlehead salad immediately, while the fiddleheads are still crisp and the flavors are fresh.

Fiddlehead salad is best enjoyed as a side dish or light lunch during the spring when fiddleheads are in season. It's a nutritious and flavorful way to highlight this unique wild vegetable, commonly found in Canadian cuisine, especially in regions like Atlantic Canada.

Chicken Pot Pie

Ingredients:

For the Pie Crust:

- 2 1/2 cups all-purpose flour
- 1 teaspoon salt
- 1 cup unsalted butter, cold and cut into cubes
- 6-8 tablespoons ice water

For the Filling:

- 4 tablespoons unsalted butter
- 1 onion, chopped
- 2 carrots, diced
- 2 celery stalks, diced
- 2 garlic cloves, minced
- 1/2 cup all-purpose flour
- 4 cups chicken broth
- 1 cup milk or heavy cream
- 4 cups cooked chicken, diced or shredded
- 1 cup frozen peas
- 1 teaspoon dried thyme (or 1 tablespoon fresh thyme leaves)
- Salt and pepper, to taste

Instructions:

1. Make the Pie Crust:
    - In a large bowl, whisk together the flour and salt.
    - Add the cold cubed butter and use a pastry cutter or your fingers to work the butter into the flour until the mixture resembles coarse crumbs.
    - Gradually add the ice water, 1 tablespoon at a time, mixing with a fork until the dough just begins to come together. It should hold together when pinched.
    - Divide the dough in half, shape each half into a disk, wrap them in plastic wrap, and refrigerate for at least 30 minutes.
2. Prepare the Filling:
    - In a large skillet or Dutch oven, melt the butter over medium heat.
    - Add the chopped onion, diced carrots, and diced celery. Cook for about 5-7 minutes, or until the vegetables are softened.

- Add the minced garlic and cook for another 1-2 minutes until fragrant.
3. **Make the Sauce:**
    - Sprinkle the flour over the vegetables and stir to combine. Cook for 1-2 minutes, stirring constantly.
    - Gradually add the chicken broth and milk (or cream), stirring constantly to avoid lumps. Bring the mixture to a simmer and cook for 5-7 minutes, or until the sauce has thickened.
4. **Add Chicken and Vegetables:**
    - Stir in the cooked chicken, frozen peas, dried thyme (or fresh thyme leaves), salt, and pepper. Remove from heat and let the filling cool slightly.
5. **Assemble and Bake:**
    - Preheat your oven to 400°F (200°C).
    - On a lightly floured surface, roll out one disk of chilled pie dough into a circle large enough to line a 9-inch pie dish. Carefully transfer the dough to the pie dish, gently pressing it into the bottom and sides.
    - Spoon the cooled chicken filling into the prepared pie crust, spreading it evenly.
    - Roll out the second disk of chilled pie dough into a circle large enough to cover the pie. Place it over the filling.
    - Trim any excess dough hanging over the edges of the pie dish. Press the edges of the top and bottom crusts together, then fold under and crimp as desired.
    - Cut a few small slits in the top crust to allow steam to escape during baking.
6. **Bake the Pie:**
    - Place the pie on a baking sheet (to catch any drips) and bake in the preheated oven for 45-50 minutes, or until the crust is golden brown and the filling is bubbling.
7. **Cool and Serve:**
    - Remove the chicken pot pie from the oven and let it cool for at least 10-15 minutes before slicing and serving.

Chicken pot pie is a comforting and hearty dish that's perfect for colder months or any time you crave a delicious homemade meal. Enjoy it with family and friends, and savor the creamy filling and flaky crust!

Maritime Seafood Chowder

Ingredients:

- 1 lb mixed seafood (such as cod, shrimp, scallops, and/or lobster), chopped into bite-sized pieces
- 4 slices bacon, chopped
- 1 onion, diced
- 2 celery stalks, diced
- 2-3 potatoes, peeled and diced
- 3 cups seafood or fish stock (can substitute with chicken or vegetable broth)
- 1 cup heavy cream
- 2 tablespoons all-purpose flour
- 2 tablespoons butter
- 1 bay leaf
- 1/2 teaspoon dried thyme
- Salt and pepper, to taste
- Chopped fresh parsley, for garnish
- Oyster crackers or crusty bread, for serving

Instructions:

1. Cook the Bacon:
   - In a large pot or Dutch oven, cook the chopped bacon over medium heat until crisp. Remove the bacon with a slotted spoon and set aside on a paper towel-lined plate.
2. Sauté Vegetables:
   - In the same pot with the bacon drippings, add the diced onion and celery. Sauté for 5-7 minutes, or until softened.
3. Make the Roux:
   - Add the butter to the pot with the onions and celery. Once melted, sprinkle in the flour and stir to create a roux. Cook for 1-2 minutes, stirring constantly, until the flour is lightly browned.
4. Add Broth and Potatoes:
   - Gradually pour in the seafood or fish stock, stirring constantly to avoid lumps from the roux. Add the bay leaf, dried thyme, and diced potatoes. Bring the mixture to a simmer.
5. Simmer the Chowder:
   - Reduce the heat to medium-low and simmer the chowder uncovered for about 15-20 minutes, or until the potatoes are tender and cooked through.

6. Add Seafood and Cream:
    - Stir in the chopped seafood (cod, shrimp, scallops, lobster) and cook for an additional 5-7 minutes, or until the seafood is cooked through.
    - Pour in the heavy cream and stir gently to combine. Season with salt and pepper to taste. Be careful not to overcook the seafood; it should be tender and just cooked through.
7. Serve:
    - Remove the bay leaf from the chowder. Ladle the Maritime Seafood Chowder into bowls.
    - Garnish with the reserved crispy bacon bits and chopped fresh parsley.
    - Serve hot, accompanied by oyster crackers or crusty bread for dipping.

Maritime Seafood Chowder is a delicious and comforting dish that highlights the flavors of the sea and the bounty of fresh seafood available in the Maritime provinces of Canada. Enjoy this hearty chowder as a main course for a satisfying meal, especially during cooler weather or as a special treat any time of the year!

Alberta Beef Stew

Ingredients:

- 2 lbs beef chuck roast, cut into 1-inch cubes
- Salt and pepper, to taste
- 2 tablespoons all-purpose flour
- 2 tablespoons vegetable oil or canola oil
- 1 large onion, diced
- 3 cloves garlic, minced
- 2 carrots, peeled and diced
- 2 celery stalks, diced
- 2 potatoes, peeled and diced
- 1 tablespoon tomato paste
- 4 cups beef broth
- 1 cup red wine (optional)
- 1 bay leaf
- 1 teaspoon dried thyme
- 1 teaspoon dried rosemary
- 1 cup frozen peas (optional)
- Chopped fresh parsley, for garnish

Instructions:

1. Prepare the Beef:
   - Season the beef cubes with salt and pepper. Dredge the beef in the flour to coat evenly, shaking off any excess.
2. Brown the Beef:
   - In a large Dutch oven or heavy-bottomed pot, heat the vegetable oil over medium-high heat. Add the beef cubes in batches and brown them on all sides. Remove the browned beef from the pot and set aside.
3. Sauté the Vegetables:
   - In the same pot, add the diced onion and cook for 3-4 minutes, until softened.
   - Add the minced garlic, diced carrots, diced celery, and diced potatoes. Sauté for another 5 minutes, stirring occasionally.
4. Deglaze the Pot:
   - Stir in the tomato paste and cook for 1-2 minutes, stirring constantly.
   - Pour in the beef broth and red wine (if using), scraping the bottom of the pot with a wooden spoon to release any browned bits.

5. Simmer the Stew:
   - Return the browned beef cubes to the pot. Add the bay leaf, dried thyme, and dried rosemary.
   - Bring the stew to a boil, then reduce the heat to low. Cover and simmer for 1.5 to 2 hours, stirring occasionally, until the beef is tender and the flavors have melded together.
6. Add the Peas (if using):
   - About 10-15 minutes before serving, stir in the frozen peas to heat through.
7. Serve:
   - Remove the bay leaf from the stew. Taste and adjust seasoning with salt and pepper if needed.
   - Ladle the Alberta Beef Stew into bowls and garnish with chopped fresh parsley.
   - Serve hot, accompanied by crusty bread or biscuits for a satisfying meal.

Alberta Beef Stew is a comforting and hearty dish perfect for colder months or any time you crave a warm and flavorful meal. It's a delicious way to enjoy the quality beef from Alberta, Canada, combined with wholesome vegetables in a rich broth.

Nova Scotia Hodge Podge

Ingredients:

- 2 cups fresh green peas (can substitute with frozen peas)
- 2 cups new potatoes, diced (about 1-inch pieces)
- 1 cup carrots, sliced
- 1 cup fresh green beans, trimmed and cut into bite-sized pieces
- 2 cups chicken or vegetable broth
- 1/2 cup heavy cream (optional)
- 2 tablespoons butter
- Salt and pepper, to taste
- Chopped fresh herbs (such as parsley or dill), for garnish

Instructions:

1. Prepare the Vegetables:
    - In a large pot, bring the chicken or vegetable broth to a boil over medium-high heat.
    - Add the diced new potatoes and sliced carrots to the boiling broth. Cook for about 5-7 minutes, or until the potatoes and carrots are just tender.
    - Add the fresh green peas and green beans to the pot. Cook for an additional 3-4 minutes, or until all the vegetables are tender-crisp. If using frozen peas, add them during the last 2 minutes of cooking.
2. Finish the Hodge Podge:
    - Drain the vegetables, reserving about 1/2 cup of the cooking liquid.
    - Return the cooked vegetables to the pot. Add the butter and heavy cream (if using), stirring gently until the butter is melted and the cream is incorporated.
    - If desired, add some of the reserved cooking liquid to achieve your desired consistency for the stew. Season with salt and pepper to taste.
3. Serve:
    - Ladle the Nova Scotia Hodge Podge into bowls.
    - Garnish with chopped fresh herbs, such as parsley or dill, for added flavor and freshness.
4. Optional Variations:
    - Some recipes may include other seasonal vegetables like turnips or summer squash.
    - For a richer flavor, you can use half-and-half or whole milk instead of heavy cream.

- Feel free to adjust the seasoning and add more butter or cream according to your taste preferences.

Nova Scotia Hodge Podge is a delightful dish that celebrates the flavors of summer vegetables, making it a perfect side dish or light meal during the warmer months. Enjoy its simplicity and freshness with locally sourced ingredients if possible, for an authentic taste of Nova Scotia cuisine.

Ontario Apple Crisp

Ingredients:

For the Apple Filling:

- 6-8 Ontario apples (such as Honeycrisp, Gala, or McIntosh), peeled, cored, and sliced
- 1/4 cup granulated sugar
- 1 tablespoon all-purpose flour
- 1 teaspoon ground cinnamon
- 1/4 teaspoon ground nutmeg
- 1 tablespoon lemon juice

For the Crisp Topping:

- 1 cup old-fashioned rolled oats
- 1/2 cup all-purpose flour
- 1/2 cup packed brown sugar
- 1/2 teaspoon ground cinnamon
- 1/4 teaspoon salt
- 1/2 cup cold unsalted butter, cut into small pieces

Instructions:

1. Preheat the Oven:
    - Preheat your oven to 350°F (175°C). Grease a 9x9-inch baking dish or a similar-sized baking dish with butter or cooking spray.
2. Prepare the Apple Filling:
    - In a large bowl, combine the sliced apples, granulated sugar, flour, ground cinnamon, ground nutmeg, and lemon juice. Toss gently to coat the apples evenly.
3. Make the Crisp Topping:
    - In another bowl, combine the rolled oats, flour, brown sugar, ground cinnamon, and salt.
    - Add the cold butter pieces to the oat mixture. Use your fingers or a pastry cutter to work the butter into the dry ingredients until the mixture resembles coarse crumbs.
4. Assemble and Bake:
    - Spread the apple mixture evenly in the prepared baking dish.
    - Sprinkle the oat topping evenly over the apples, covering them completely.

5. Bake the Apple Crisp:
    - Place the baking dish in the preheated oven and bake for 40-45 minutes, or until the apple filling is bubbly and the topping is golden brown and crisp.
6. Serve:
    - Remove the Ontario Apple Crisp from the oven and let it cool slightly.
    - Serve warm, optionally with a scoop of vanilla ice cream or a dollop of whipped cream.

Enjoy the Ontario Apple Crisp as a delicious dessert that highlights the flavors of locally grown apples. It's perfect for family gatherings, holidays, or any time you want to indulge in a comforting treat that celebrates the autumn harvest of apples in Ontario.

Quebec Sugar Pie (Tarte au Sucre)

Ingredients:

For the Pie Crust:

- 1 1/4 cups all-purpose flour
- 1/2 teaspoon salt
- 1/2 cup unsalted butter, cold and cut into cubes
- 4-5 tablespoons ice water

For the Filling:

- 1 cup packed brown sugar (light or dark)
- 1/2 cup heavy cream (35% whipping cream)
- 1/4 cup unsalted butter, melted
- 2 tablespoons all-purpose flour
- 1 teaspoon vanilla extract
- Pinch of salt

Instructions:

1. Make the Pie Crust:
    - In a large bowl, whisk together the flour and salt.
    - Add the cold cubed butter to the flour mixture. Use a pastry cutter or your fingers to work the butter into the flour until the mixture resembles coarse crumbs.
    - Gradually add the ice water, 1 tablespoon at a time, mixing with a fork until the dough just begins to come together. It should hold together when pinched.
    - Gather the dough into a ball, flatten it into a disk, wrap it in plastic wrap, and refrigerate for at least 30 minutes.
2. Preheat the Oven:
    - Preheat your oven to 375°F (190°C). Lightly grease a 9-inch pie dish.
3. Roll Out the Pie Crust:
    - On a lightly floured surface, roll out the chilled dough into a circle about 12 inches in diameter. Carefully transfer the dough to the prepared pie dish, pressing it gently into the bottom and up the sides. Trim any excess dough and crimp the edges as desired.
4. Prepare the Filling:

- In a medium bowl, whisk together the brown sugar, heavy cream, melted butter, flour, vanilla extract, and salt until smooth and well combined.
5. Assemble and Bake:
    - Pour the filling into the prepared pie crust.
    - Place the pie dish on a baking sheet (to catch any drips) and bake in the preheated oven for 40-45 minutes, or until the filling is set and golden brown on top. The center may still jiggle slightly, but it will continue to set as it cools.
6. Cool and Serve:
    - Remove the Quebec Sugar Pie from the oven and let it cool completely on a wire rack before slicing and serving.
    - Serve the pie at room temperature or slightly warmed, optionally with a dollop of whipped cream or a scoop of vanilla ice cream.

Quebec Sugar Pie (Tarte au Sucre) is a delightful dessert that showcases the rich flavors of brown sugar and cream, encased in a buttery pie crust. It's a beloved treat in Quebec cuisine, perfect for special occasions or any time you crave a sweet and indulgent dessert.

Wild Rice and Mushroom Pilaf

Ingredients:

- 1 cup wild rice
- 2 cups chicken or vegetable broth
- 1 tablespoon olive oil or butter
- 1 onion, finely chopped
- 2 garlic cloves, minced
- 8 oz mushrooms (such as cremini or button), sliced
- 1/2 teaspoon dried thyme (or 1 teaspoon fresh thyme leaves)
- 1/2 teaspoon dried sage
- Salt and pepper, to taste
- 1/4 cup chopped fresh parsley, for garnish (optional)

Instructions:

1. Prepare the Wild Rice:
    - Rinse the wild rice under cold water in a fine mesh sieve.
    - In a medium saucepan, bring the chicken or vegetable broth to a boil.
    - Add the rinsed wild rice to the boiling broth. Reduce heat to low, cover, and simmer for about 45-50 minutes, or until the wild rice is tender and has absorbed most of the liquid. Remove from heat and let it stand covered for 5-10 minutes.
2. Sauté the Vegetables:
    - While the wild rice is cooking, heat the olive oil or butter in a large skillet over medium heat.
    - Add the chopped onion and cook for 3-4 minutes, or until softened and translucent.
    - Add the minced garlic and cook for another 1-2 minutes until fragrant.
3. Cook the Mushrooms:
    - Add the sliced mushrooms to the skillet with the onions and garlic. Cook for 5-7 minutes, or until the mushrooms are tender and browned, stirring occasionally.
4. Combine and Season:
    - Stir in the cooked wild rice to the skillet with the mushrooms and onions.
    - Add the dried thyme, dried sage, salt, and pepper to taste. Stir well to combine and heat through.
5. Serve:
    - Transfer the Wild Rice and Mushroom Pilaf to a serving dish.

- Garnish with chopped fresh parsley, if desired, before serving.

Wild Rice and Mushroom Pilaf is a versatile dish that can be served as a side dish alongside roasted meats or as a vegetarian main dish. It's packed with flavor and textures that make it perfect for any occasion, from weeknight dinners to holiday gatherings. Enjoy its hearty goodness and earthy flavors!

Bison Burgers

Ingredients:

- 1 lb ground bison meat
- 1 small onion, finely chopped (optional)
- 2 cloves garlic, minced
- 1 tablespoon Worcestershire sauce
- 1 teaspoon Dijon mustard
- 1/2 teaspoon smoked paprika
- Salt and pepper, to taste
- 4 burger buns
- Your choice of toppings (lettuce, tomato, onion, cheese, etc.)
- Olive oil or vegetable oil, for cooking

Instructions:

1. Prepare the Bison Burger Patties:
    - In a large bowl, combine the ground bison meat, finely chopped onion (if using), minced garlic, Worcestershire sauce, Dijon mustard, smoked paprika, salt, and pepper.
    - Mix the ingredients gently but thoroughly, being careful not to overwork the meat.
    - Divide the mixture into 4 equal portions and shape each portion into a patty, about 1/2 to 3/4 inch thick. Make a slight indentation in the center of each patty with your thumb to prevent it from puffing up while cooking.
2. Cook the Bison Burgers:
    - Heat a grill pan, skillet, or outdoor grill over medium-high heat. Brush with olive oil or vegetable oil to prevent sticking.
    - Place the bison burger patties on the hot grill or skillet. Cook for about 4-5 minutes on each side, or until the burgers reach your desired level of doneness (internal temperature of 160°F for medium).
    - Avoid pressing down on the patties with a spatula while cooking, as this can squeeze out juices and make the burgers less juicy.
3. Assemble the Bison Burgers:
    - Toast the burger buns lightly on the grill or in a toaster.
    - Place each cooked bison burger patty on a toasted bun.
    - Add your favorite toppings such as lettuce, tomato slices, onion rings, cheese, and condiments.
    - Serve the Bison Burgers immediately while hot and enjoy!

Bison burgers are best served with your favorite side dishes like sweet potato fries, coleslaw, or a fresh green salad. They offer a leaner alternative to beef burgers with a unique and delicious flavor that pairs well with a variety of toppings and condiments.

Prairie Perogies

Ingredients:

For the Dough:

- 2 cups all-purpose flour
- 1/2 teaspoon salt
- 1 large egg
- 1/2 cup sour cream
- 4 tablespoons unsalted butter, softened
- 1/4 cup water (as needed)

For the Filling:

- 2 cups mashed potatoes (about 3-4 medium potatoes, boiled and mashed)
- 1 cup shredded cheddar cheese
- Salt and pepper, to taste
- Optional: caramelized onions, bacon bits, or other fillings of your choice

For Serving:

- 1/2 cup unsalted butter
- Sour cream, for serving
- Chopped chives or green onions, for garnish

Instructions:

1. Prepare the Dough:
    - In a large bowl, whisk together the flour and salt.
    - In a separate bowl, whisk together the egg, sour cream, and softened butter until smooth.
    - Gradually add the wet ingredients to the flour mixture, stirring with a wooden spoon or your hands, until the dough comes together. If the dough is too dry, add water, 1 tablespoon at a time, until it forms a smooth and elastic dough.
    - Knead the dough on a lightly floured surface for about 5 minutes, until smooth. Wrap the dough in plastic wrap and let it rest at room temperature for 30 minutes.
2. Make the Filling:

- In a bowl, combine the mashed potatoes and shredded cheddar cheese. Season with salt and pepper to taste. Mix well.
- Optionally, you can add caramelized onions, bacon bits, or other fillings of your choice to the potato mixture for added flavor.

3. Assemble the Perogies:
    - Roll out the rested dough on a lightly floured surface to about 1/8 inch thickness.
    - Use a round cookie cutter or a drinking glass to cut out circles of dough, about 3 inches in diameter.
    - Place a small spoonful of the potato filling in the center of each dough circle.
    - Fold the dough over the filling to form a half-moon shape. Press the edges firmly to seal, using a fork to crimp the edges if desired.
4. Cook the Perogies:
    - Bring a large pot of salted water to a boil.
    - Carefully drop the perogies into the boiling water, a few at a time, and cook for about 3-4 minutes, or until they float to the surface.
    - Remove the perogies with a slotted spoon and transfer them to a plate.
5. Serve the Perogies:
    - In a skillet, melt the unsalted butter over medium heat until it begins to bubble.
    - Add the cooked perogies to the skillet in a single layer. Fry the perogies for 2-3 minutes on each side, or until golden and crisp.
    - Serve the prairie perogies hot, drizzled with melted butter and topped with sour cream and chopped chives or green onions.

Prairie perogies are a comforting and delicious dish that can be enjoyed as a main course or as a side dish. They are perfect for gatherings, family meals, or any time you crave a taste of Canadian comfort food!

Calgary Ginger Beef

Ingredients:

For the Beef:

- 1 lb flank steak, thinly sliced against the grain
- 1/2 cup cornstarch
- Vegetable oil, for frying

For the Ginger Sauce:

- 1/4 cup soy sauce
- 1/4 cup water
- 1/4 cup rice vinegar
- 1/4 cup granulated sugar
- 2 tablespoons hoisin sauce
- 1 tablespoon fresh ginger, minced
- 2 cloves garlic, minced
- 1 tablespoon cornstarch mixed with 2 tablespoons water (slurry)
- 1 green onion, thinly sliced (for garnish)
- Sesame seeds (for garnish, optional)

Instructions:

1. Prepare the Beef:
   - Place the thinly sliced flank steak in a bowl and toss with 1/2 cup of cornstarch until evenly coated.
   - Heat vegetable oil in a large skillet or wok over medium-high heat.
   - Working in batches, fry the coated beef strips until crispy and golden brown, about 2-3 minutes per batch. Remove the beef with a slotted spoon and place on a paper towel-lined plate to drain excess oil. Set aside.
2. Make the Ginger Sauce:
   - In a small bowl, whisk together soy sauce, water, rice vinegar, sugar, hoisin sauce, minced ginger, and minced garlic.
   - Pour the sauce mixture into a saucepan and bring to a simmer over medium heat.
   - Gradually stir in the cornstarch slurry (cornstarch mixed with water), stirring constantly until the sauce thickens to desired consistency, about 2-3 minutes.
3. Combine and Serve:

- Add the crispy beef strips to the simmering sauce, tossing gently to coat evenly.
- Cook for an additional 1-2 minutes, allowing the beef to absorb the flavors of the sauce.
- Remove from heat and garnish with sliced green onions and sesame seeds, if desired.

4. Serve Calgary Ginger Beef:
    - Serve hot Calgary Ginger Beef over steamed rice or noodles.
    - Enjoy this delicious and flavorful Canadian-Chinese dish!

Calgary Ginger Beef is known for its crispy texture and the perfect balance of sweet and savory flavors from the ginger sauce. It's a delightful dish that captures the essence of fusion cuisine and is sure to be a hit at any dinner table.

Atlantic Cod Cakes

Ingredients:

- 1 lb fresh Atlantic cod fillets, cooked and flaked (about 2 cups)
- 1/2 cup breadcrumbs (plus extra for coating)
- 1/4 cup mayonnaise
- 1 egg, lightly beaten
- 1 tablespoon Dijon mustard
- 2 tablespoons chopped fresh parsley
- 2 green onions, finely chopped
- 1 garlic clove, minced
- 1/2 teaspoon Old Bay seasoning (or seafood seasoning of choice)
- Salt and pepper, to taste
- Vegetable oil, for frying

For Serving:

- Lemon wedges
- Tartar sauce or aioli

Instructions:

1. Prepare the Cod:
    - Cook the cod fillets by poaching, baking, or steaming until fully cooked and flakey. Let them cool slightly, then flake the fish into small pieces using a fork.
2. Make the Cod Cake Mixture:
    - In a large bowl, combine the flaked cod, breadcrumbs, mayonnaise, beaten egg, Dijon mustard, chopped parsley, chopped green onions, minced garlic, Old Bay seasoning, salt, and pepper. Mix well until all ingredients are evenly combined.
3. Form the Cod Cakes:
    - Divide the mixture into equal portions and shape each portion into a round patty, about 3 inches in diameter and 1/2 inch thick.
    - Coat each cod cake lightly with additional breadcrumbs, pressing gently to adhere. This helps to form a crispy crust when frying.
4. Cook the Cod Cakes:
    - Heat vegetable oil in a large skillet over medium heat.

- Carefully place the cod cakes in the hot skillet, working in batches if necessary to avoid overcrowding.
- Fry the cod cakes for about 3-4 minutes on each side, or until golden brown and crispy. Use a spatula to carefully flip them halfway through cooking.

5. Serve:
    - Remove the cod cakes from the skillet and place them on a paper towel-lined plate to drain excess oil.
    - Serve the Atlantic Cod Cakes hot, garnished with lemon wedges and accompanied by tartar sauce or aioli for dipping.

Atlantic Cod Cakes are flavorful, tender on the inside, and crispy on the outside. They are perfect as an appetizer, light lunch, or part of a seafood-themed dinner. Enjoy these delicious cod cakes with your favorite sides or on their own for a taste of Atlantic seafood goodness!

Ontario Corn Chowder

Ingredients:

- 4 cups fresh corn kernels (about 4-5 ears of corn)
- 4 slices bacon, chopped
- 1 onion, diced
- 2 cloves garlic, minced
- 2 medium potatoes, peeled and diced
- 2 cups chicken or vegetable broth
- 1 cup milk or cream (or a combination for desired richness)
- 1/2 teaspoon dried thyme
- 1/2 teaspoon smoked paprika
- Salt and pepper, to taste
- Chopped fresh parsley or chives, for garnish

Instructions:

1. Prepare the Corn:
   - Cut the kernels off the corn cobs. Reserve about 1 cup of corn kernels for later.
2. Cook the Bacon and Onions:
   - In a large pot or Dutch oven, cook the chopped bacon over medium heat until crispy. Remove the bacon with a slotted spoon and set aside on a paper towel-lined plate.
   - In the same pot with the bacon drippings, add the diced onion. Cook for 3-4 minutes until softened and translucent.
3. Add Garlic and Potatoes:
   - Add the minced garlic to the pot and cook for another minute until fragrant.
   - Add the diced potatoes and cook for 3-4 minutes, stirring occasionally.
4. Simmer the Chowder:
   - Pour in the chicken or vegetable broth and bring to a boil.
   - Reduce the heat to medium-low and simmer uncovered for about 10-12 minutes, or until the potatoes are tender.
5. Blend the Chowder (optional):
   - If you prefer a smoother texture, use an immersion blender to blend part of the soup until creamy, leaving some chunks of potatoes for texture.
6. Add Corn and Seasonings:

- Add the remaining corn kernels, dried thyme, smoked paprika, salt, and pepper to the pot. Stir to combine.
- Cook for another 5 minutes, allowing the corn to cook through.
7. Finish the Chowder:
    - Stir in the milk or cream (or a combination) to the pot. Adjust the consistency with more broth or milk if needed.
    - Taste and adjust seasoning with salt and pepper as desired.
8. Serve:
    - Ladle the Ontario Corn Chowder into bowls.
    - Garnish with the crispy bacon, chopped fresh parsley or chives.
    - Serve hot, optionally with crusty bread or cornbread on the side.

Enjoy this creamy and flavorful Ontario Corn Chowder, highlighting the fresh sweetness of corn and complemented by smoky bacon and savory seasonings. It's a perfect dish to savor during late summer or early fall when Ontario corn is at its peak!

Manitoba Cabbage Rolls

Ingredients:

For the Cabbage Rolls:

- 1 large head of cabbage
- 1 lb ground beef
- 1/2 lb ground pork
- 1 cup cooked rice
- 1 onion, finely chopped
- 2 cloves garlic, minced
- 1 egg
- 1/4 cup milk
- 1 teaspoon salt
- 1/2 teaspoon black pepper
- 1/2 teaspoon paprika
- 1/4 teaspoon dried thyme
- 1/4 teaspoon dried dill (optional)
- 1/4 cup chopped fresh parsley
- 1 tablespoon vegetable oil

For the Tomato Sauce:

- 2 cups tomato sauce or crushed tomatoes
- 1 cup beef broth or water
- 1 tablespoon brown sugar
- 1 tablespoon cider vinegar
- Salt and pepper, to taste

Instructions:

1. Prepare the Cabbage:
    - Bring a large pot of salted water to a boil. Carefully remove any damaged outer leaves from the cabbage head.
    - Place the whole cabbage head in the boiling water and cook for about 5 minutes, or until the outer leaves are tender enough to peel off easily with tongs. Remove the cabbage from the water and let it cool slightly.
    - Carefully peel off about 12 large cabbage leaves, trimming the thick center vein to make them easier to roll. Set the leaves aside.
2. Make the Filling:

- In a large bowl, combine the ground beef, ground pork, cooked rice, finely chopped onion, minced garlic, egg, milk, salt, pepper, paprika, dried thyme, dried dill (if using), and chopped fresh parsley. Mix well until all ingredients are evenly incorporated.
3. Assemble the Cabbage Rolls:
    - Place a cabbage leaf on a clean surface. Spoon about 1/4 to 1/3 cup of the meat and rice mixture onto the center of the leaf, depending on the size of the leaf. Fold the sides of the leaf over the filling, then roll it up tightly, tucking in the sides as you go. Repeat with the remaining cabbage leaves and filling.
4. Cook the Cabbage Rolls:
    - In a large pot or Dutch oven, heat the vegetable oil over medium heat. Arrange the cabbage rolls seam side down in the pot.
    - In a bowl, whisk together the tomato sauce or crushed tomatoes, beef broth or water, brown sugar, cider vinegar, salt, and pepper. Pour the sauce over the cabbage rolls, covering them evenly.
    - Bring the sauce to a simmer over medium-low heat. Cover the pot with a lid and cook for about 1.5 to 2 hours, or until the cabbage rolls are tender and fully cooked, and the flavors have melded. Stir gently occasionally to ensure even cooking and prevent sticking.
5. Serve:
    - Carefully transfer the Manitoba Cabbage Rolls to serving plates using a slotted spoon.
    - Serve hot, spooning the tomato sauce over the rolls. Optionally, garnish with additional chopped parsley or dill.

Manitoba Cabbage Rolls are a comforting and satisfying dish that can be served as a main course with crusty bread or mashed potatoes. They are perfect for gatherings and celebrations, offering a taste of hearty Eastern European cuisine with tender cabbage and flavorful meat filling.

Quebecois Tourtière

Ingredients:

For the Pastry:

- 2 1/2 cups all-purpose flour
- 1 teaspoon salt
- 1 cup unsalted butter, cold and cut into cubes
- 6-8 tablespoons ice water

For the Filling:

- 1 lb ground pork (or a mixture of pork and beef)
- 1 onion, finely chopped
- 2 cloves garlic, minced
- 1/2 teaspoon ground cinnamon
- 1/4 teaspoon ground cloves
- 1/4 teaspoon ground allspice
- 1/4 teaspoon ground nutmeg
- Salt and pepper, to taste
- 1/2 cup chicken or beef broth
- 1/2 cup breadcrumbs (optional, for binding)
- Egg wash (1 egg beaten with 1 tablespoon water), for brushing

Instructions:

1. Prepare the Pastry:
    - In a large bowl, whisk together the flour and salt.
    - Add the cold cubed butter to the flour mixture. Use a pastry cutter or your fingers to work the butter into the flour until the mixture resembles coarse crumbs.
    - Gradually add the ice water, 1 tablespoon at a time, mixing with a fork until the dough just begins to come together. It should hold together when pinched.
    - Gather the dough into a ball, divide it into two equal portions, flatten each portion into a disk, wrap them in plastic wrap, and refrigerate for at least 30 minutes.
2. Make the Filling:

- In a large skillet or frying pan, cook the ground pork (or pork and beef mixture) over medium heat until browned and cooked through, breaking up any large chunks with a spoon.
- Add the chopped onion and minced garlic to the skillet with the cooked meat. Cook for 3-4 minutes until the onion is softened and translucent.
- Stir in the ground cinnamon, ground cloves, ground allspice, ground nutmeg, salt, and pepper. Cook for another minute until fragrant.
- Add the chicken or beef broth to the skillet, stirring to combine. Reduce the heat to low and simmer for 10-15 minutes, allowing the flavors to meld and the mixture to thicken slightly. If needed, stir in breadcrumbs to bind the filling. Remove from heat and let cool slightly.

3. Assemble the Tourtière:
   - Preheat your oven to 375°F (190°C).
   - On a lightly floured surface, roll out one disk of chilled pastry dough into a circle about 12 inches in diameter. Carefully transfer the rolled dough to a 9-inch pie dish or deep dish pie pan.
   - Spoon the cooled meat filling into the pastry-lined dish, spreading it evenly.
   - Roll out the second disk of chilled pastry dough into a circle about 12 inches in diameter. Place it over the filled pie dish.
   - Trim any excess dough and crimp the edges of the pastry to seal. Cut a few small slits in the top pastry crust to allow steam to escape during baking.

4. Bake the Tourtière:
   - Brush the top of the pie with the egg wash for a golden finish.
   - Place the tourtière in the preheated oven and bake for 45-50 minutes, or until the crust is golden brown and the filling is heated through.

5. Serve:
   - Remove the Quebecois Tourtière from the oven and let it cool for 10-15 minutes before slicing and serving.
   - Serve warm slices of tourtière with your favorite accompaniments such as cranberry sauce, pickles, or a side salad.

Quebecois Tourtière is a classic Canadian dish that is cherished for its hearty flavors and festive appeal. It's perfect for holiday gatherings or any time you want to enjoy a comforting, traditional meat pie.

Wild Blueberry Pancakes

Ingredients:

- 1 cup all-purpose flour
- 1 tablespoon granulated sugar
- 1 teaspoon baking powder
- 1/2 teaspoon baking soda
- 1/4 teaspoon salt
- 1 cup buttermilk
- 1 large egg
- 2 tablespoons unsalted butter, melted
- 1 teaspoon vanilla extract
- 1 cup wild blueberries (fresh or frozen)
- Butter or oil, for cooking pancakes

Instructions:

1. Prepare the Dry Ingredients:
    - In a large bowl, whisk together the flour, sugar, baking powder, baking soda, and salt until well combined.
2. Mix the Wet Ingredients:
    - In another bowl, whisk together the buttermilk, egg, melted butter, and vanilla extract until smooth.
3. Combine Wet and Dry Ingredients:
    - Pour the wet ingredients into the bowl with the dry ingredients. Stir gently with a spatula or wooden spoon until just combined. The batter may be slightly lumpy, which is okay. Do not overmix.
4. Fold in Blueberries:
    - Gently fold the wild blueberries into the pancake batter. If using frozen blueberries, toss them with a tablespoon of flour before folding into the batter to prevent them from sinking to the bottom.
5. Cook the Pancakes:
    - Heat a large non-stick skillet or griddle over medium heat. Add a small amount of butter or oil and swirl to coat the surface.
    - Pour about 1/4 cup of batter onto the skillet for each pancake, spreading it slightly with the back of a spoon to form a round shape.
    - Cook the pancakes for about 2-3 minutes, or until bubbles form on the surface and the edges look set.

- 6. Serve:
    - Flip the pancakes with a spatula and cook for another 1-2 minutes, or until golden brown and cooked through.
    - Transfer the cooked pancakes to a plate and keep warm.
    - Repeat with the remaining batter, adding more butter or oil to the skillet as needed.
- 7. Enjoy:
    - Serve the Wild Blueberry Pancakes warm, topped with maple syrup, additional fresh blueberries, a dollop of whipped cream, or your favorite pancake toppings.

These Wild Blueberry Pancakes are fluffy, flavorful, and bursting with the natural sweetness of wild blueberries. They are perfect for a leisurely weekend breakfast or brunch, bringing a taste of fresh berries to your morning table.

B.C. Spot Prawns

Ingredients:

- 1 lb B.C. Spot Prawns, peeled and deveined
- 2 tablespoons olive oil
- 2 cloves garlic, minced
- Zest and juice of 1 lemon
- Salt and pepper, to taste
- Fresh parsley or cilantro, chopped (for garnish)
- Lemon wedges, for serving

Instructions:

1. Prepare the Prawns:
    - If not already done, peel and devein the B.C. Spot Prawns, leaving the tails intact for presentation.
2. Marinate the Prawns:
    - In a bowl, combine the olive oil, minced garlic, lemon zest, lemon juice, salt, and pepper.
    - Add the peeled and deveined prawns to the marinade, tossing gently to coat evenly. Let the prawns marinate for about 15-20 minutes at room temperature.
3. Preheat the Grill:
    - Preheat an outdoor grill or grill pan over medium-high heat. Brush the grill grates with oil to prevent sticking.
4. Grill the Prawns:
    - Thread the marinated prawns onto skewers, if desired, or grill them directly on the grates.
    - Grill the prawns for 2-3 minutes on each side, or until they are opaque and cooked through. Avoid overcooking to maintain their delicate texture.
5. Serve:
    - Transfer the grilled B.C. Spot Prawns to a serving platter.
    - Sprinkle with chopped fresh parsley or cilantro for garnish.
    - Serve immediately with lemon wedges on the side for squeezing over the prawns.

Tips for Serving B.C. Spot Prawns:

- Butter and Garlic Sauce: Serve grilled spot prawns with a side of melted butter infused with minced garlic and a squeeze of lemon juice.
- Salad: Add grilled spot prawns to a fresh green salad for a light and refreshing meal.
- Pasta: Toss grilled spot prawns with pasta, olive oil, garlic, and cherry tomatoes for a simple yet flavorful pasta dish.

Grilled B.C. Spot Prawns are a delicious way to enjoy the natural sweetness and tender texture of these prized seafood delicacies. Whether enjoyed as a main dish or part of a larger meal, they are sure to impress with their fresh and vibrant flavors.

Alberta Bison Chili

Ingredients:

- 1 lb ground bison meat
- 1 tablespoon olive oil
- 1 onion, chopped
- 3 cloves garlic, minced
- 1 bell pepper, diced (any color)
- 1 jalapeño pepper, seeded and minced (optional, for heat)
- 1 can (15 oz) kidney beans, drained and rinsed
- 1 can (15 oz) black beans, drained and rinsed
- 1 can (28 oz) diced tomatoes
- 2 cups beef broth
- 2 tablespoons tomato paste
- 2 tablespoons chili powder
- 1 teaspoon ground cumin
- 1 teaspoon smoked paprika
- 1/2 teaspoon dried oregano
- Salt and pepper, to taste
- Fresh cilantro, chopped (for garnish)
- Sour cream, shredded cheese, and sliced green onions, for serving (optional)

Instructions:

1. Brown the Bison:
    - In a large pot or Dutch oven, heat olive oil over medium-high heat. Add the ground bison meat and cook until browned, breaking up the meat with a spoon as it cooks.
2. Saute Vegetables:
    - Add chopped onion, minced garlic, diced bell pepper, and minced jalapeño (if using) to the pot. Cook for 5-7 minutes, stirring occasionally, until the vegetables are softened.
3. Add Beans and Tomatoes:
    - Stir in the drained and rinsed kidney beans and black beans.
    - Add the diced tomatoes (with their juices) to the pot.
4. Season and Simmer:
    - Pour in the beef broth and stir in the tomato paste, chili powder, ground cumin, smoked paprika, dried oregano, salt, and pepper.

    - Bring the chili to a boil, then reduce the heat to low. Cover and simmer for 30-40 minutes, stirring occasionally, to allow the flavors to meld and the chili to thicken.
5. Adjust Seasoning and Serve:
    - Taste the chili and adjust seasoning with salt and pepper if needed.
    - Serve hot, garnished with chopped fresh cilantro. Optionally, top with a dollop of sour cream, shredded cheese, and sliced green onions.

Tips for Serving Alberta Bison Chili:

- **Make Ahead:** Bison chili tastes even better the next day as the flavors continue to develop. Store leftovers in the refrigerator for up to 3-4 days or freeze for longer storage.
- **Side Dishes:** Serve with cornbread, rice, or tortilla chips for dipping and scooping.
- **Customize:** Adjust the heat level by adding more or less chili powder and jalapeño peppers according to your preference.

Alberta Bison Chili is a comforting and nutritious dish that highlights the unique flavor of bison meat. It's perfect for chilly evenings or game day gatherings, offering a satisfying meal with a taste of Alberta's culinary heritage.

Maple Butter Tart Cheesecake

Ingredients:

For the Crust:

- 1 1/2 cups graham cracker crumbs
- 1/4 cup granulated sugar
- 1/2 cup unsalted butter, melted

For the Filling:

- 3 packages (8 oz each) cream cheese, softened
- 1 cup granulated sugar
- 3 large eggs
- 1/2 cup sour cream
- 1/4 cup pure maple syrup
- 1 teaspoon vanilla extract

For the Maple Butter Tart Topping:

- 1 cup packed brown sugar
- 1/2 cup unsalted butter
- 1/2 cup pure maple syrup
- 2 large eggs
- 1 teaspoon vanilla extract
- 1/2 cup chopped pecans or walnuts (optional)

Instructions:

1. Prepare the Crust:
    - Preheat your oven to 350°F (175°C). Grease a 9-inch springform pan.
    - In a bowl, combine the graham cracker crumbs, sugar, and melted butter. Press the mixture firmly into the bottom of the prepared pan. Bake for 8-10 minutes, then remove from the oven and let cool.
2. Make the Cheesecake Filling:
    - In a large bowl, beat the cream cheese and sugar together until smooth and creamy.
    - Add the eggs one at a time, beating well after each addition.
    - Stir in the sour cream, maple syrup, and vanilla extract until well combined.
3. Prepare the Maple Butter Tart Topping:

- In a saucepan, combine the brown sugar, butter, and maple syrup over medium heat. Bring to a boil, stirring constantly.
- Remove from heat and let cool slightly.
- In a separate bowl, whisk together the eggs and vanilla extract. Slowly pour the warm sugar mixture into the egg mixture, whisking constantly to temper the eggs.
- Stir in the chopped nuts, if using.

4. **Assemble and Bake:**
   - Pour the cheesecake filling over the cooled crust in the springform pan, spreading it evenly.
   - Carefully spoon the maple butter tart topping over the cheesecake filling, spreading it gently to cover the surface.

5. **Bake the Cheesecake:**
   - Place the cheesecake in the preheated oven and bake for 45-50 minutes, or until the center is set and the edges are lightly golden.
   - Turn off the oven and let the cheesecake cool in the oven with the door slightly ajar for 1 hour.

6. **Chill and Serve:**
   - Remove the cheesecake from the oven and let it cool completely at room temperature.
   - Refrigerate the cheesecake for at least 4 hours or overnight before serving.

7. **Serve:**
   - Carefully remove the sides of the springform pan before serving.
   - Slice the Maple Butter Tart Cheesecake and serve chilled. Optionally, drizzle with additional maple syrup and garnish with whipped cream or a sprinkle of chopped nuts.

This Maple Butter Tart Cheesecake combines the best of both worlds: the creamy texture of cheesecake with the rich, caramelized flavors of maple butter tart topping. It's a decadent dessert that celebrates Canadian flavors and is sure to impress at any gathering or special occasion.

Maritime Fish Cakes

Ingredients:

- 1 lb white fish fillets (such as cod, haddock, or halibut)
- 2 cups mashed potatoes (about 3-4 medium potatoes, peeled, boiled, and mashed)
- 1 small onion, finely chopped
- 2 cloves garlic, minced
- 1/4 cup fresh parsley, chopped
- 1/4 cup green onions, chopped
- 1 tablespoon lemon juice
- Zest of 1 lemon
- 1 teaspoon Dijon mustard
- 1/2 teaspoon Old Bay seasoning (or seafood seasoning of choice)
- Salt and pepper, to taste
- 1/2 cup all-purpose flour, for dredging
- 2 eggs, beaten
- 1/2 cup breadcrumbs (preferably panko breadcrumbs) or crushed saltine crackers
- Vegetable oil, for frying

Instructions:

1. Prepare the Fish:
   - Poach or steam the fish fillets until they are cooked through and easily flake with a fork. Let the fish cool slightly, then flake it into small pieces using a fork.
2. Mix the Ingredients:
   - In a large bowl, combine the flaked fish, mashed potatoes, finely chopped onion, minced garlic, chopped parsley, chopped green onions, lemon juice, lemon zest, Dijon mustard, Old Bay seasoning, salt, and pepper. Mix until well combined.
3. Shape the Fish Cakes:
   - Using your hands, shape the fish mixture into small patties, about 2-3 inches in diameter and 1/2 inch thick.
4. Coat and Dredge:
   - Dredge each fish cake in flour, shaking off any excess.
   - Dip the floured fish cakes into the beaten eggs, then coat them evenly with breadcrumbs or crushed crackers, pressing gently to adhere.

5. Fry the Fish Cakes:
    - In a large skillet or frying pan, heat enough vegetable oil to cover the bottom of the pan over medium heat.
    - Carefully place the fish cakes in the hot oil, cooking in batches if necessary to avoid overcrowding.
    - Fry the fish cakes for about 3-4 minutes per side, or until they are golden brown and crispy. Adjust the heat as needed to maintain a steady frying temperature.
6. Serve:
    - Transfer the cooked Maritime Fish Cakes to a plate lined with paper towels to drain excess oil.
    - Serve the fish cakes hot, optionally with tartar sauce, lemon wedges, or a side of coleslaw.

Tips for Serving Maritime Fish Cakes:

- Make-Ahead: Prepare the fish cakes up to the dredging stage and refrigerate them until ready to fry. This makes them a convenient option for quick meals or entertaining.
- Variations: Feel free to customize the seasoning and herbs according to your preference. Some recipes also include a dash of hot sauce or Worcestershire sauce for added flavor.

Maritime Fish Cakes are a delicious way to enjoy fresh seafood, and they reflect the maritime culinary tradition with their simple yet satisfying preparation. They make a wonderful main dish or appetizer, perfect for any seafood lover.

Quebec Maple Sugar Pie

Ingredients:

For the Pie Crust:

- 1 1/4 cups all-purpose flour
- 1/2 teaspoon salt
- 1/2 cup unsalted butter, chilled and cut into small pieces
- 2-4 tablespoons ice water

For the Filling:

- 1 cup pure maple syrup
- 1 cup heavy cream
- 1/2 cup packed brown sugar
- 2 tablespoons all-purpose flour
- 2 tablespoons unsalted butter, melted
- 1 teaspoon vanilla extract
- Pinch of salt

Instructions:

1. Prepare the Pie Crust:
    - In a large bowl, combine the flour and salt. Add the chilled butter pieces.
    - Use a pastry cutter or your fingers to work the butter into the flour until the mixture resembles coarse crumbs.
    - Gradually add the ice water, 1 tablespoon at a time, mixing with a fork until the dough just begins to come together.
    - Gather the dough into a ball, flatten into a disk, wrap it in plastic wrap, and refrigerate for at least 30 minutes.
2. Preheat the Oven:
    - Preheat your oven to 375°F (190°C).
3. Roll out the Pie Crust:
    - On a lightly floured surface, roll out the chilled dough into a circle about 12 inches in diameter.
    - Carefully transfer the rolled dough to a 9-inch pie dish. Trim any excess dough and crimp the edges as desired. Place the pie crust in the refrigerator while preparing the filling.
4. Make the Filling:

- In a medium bowl, whisk together the maple syrup, heavy cream, brown sugar, flour, melted butter, vanilla extract, and a pinch of salt until smooth and well combined.
5. Assemble and Bake:
    - Pour the filling into the chilled pie crust.
    - Place the pie on a baking sheet to catch any drips, and then carefully transfer it to the preheated oven.
    - Bake for 45-50 minutes, or until the filling is set and the crust is golden brown. The center of the pie may still jiggle slightly, but it will firm up as it cools.
6. Cool and Serve:
    - Remove the pie from the oven and let it cool completely on a wire rack before serving.
    - Serve slices of Quebec Maple Sugar Pie at room temperature or slightly warmed, optionally topped with whipped cream or a scoop of vanilla ice cream.

Tips for Quebec Maple Sugar Pie:

- Maple Syrup: Use pure maple syrup for the best flavor. Grade A or Grade B maple syrup works well in this recipe.
- Baking: To prevent the pie crust edges from over-browning, you can cover them with aluminum foil or a pie crust shield halfway through baking.
- Storage: Store any leftovers in the refrigerator. The pie can be reheated gently in the oven or microwave before serving.

Quebec Maple Sugar Pie is a delightful dessert that showcases the natural sweetness of maple syrup in a rich and creamy filling. It's perfect for special occasions or anytime you want to enjoy a taste of Canadian culinary tradition.

Canadian Club Caesar Cocktail

Ingredients:

- 1.5 oz Canadian Club whisky
- 4 oz Clamato juice (or to taste)
- 1 dash hot sauce (such as Tabasco)
- 1 dash Worcestershire sauce
- Celery salt, to rim the glass
- Freshly ground black pepper
- Ice cubes
- Celery stalk or pickled asparagus spear, for garnish
- Lemon wedge, for garnish
- Optional: Lime wedge, horseradish, or pickled beans for additional garnish

Instructions:

1. Rim the Glass:
    - Rub a lemon wedge around the rim of a highball glass to moisten it.
    - Dip the moistened rim into celery salt to coat evenly.
2. Mix the Cocktail:
    - Fill the glass with ice cubes.
    - Add Canadian Club whisky, Clamato juice, hot sauce, Worcestershire sauce, and a pinch of freshly ground black pepper.
3. Stir Well:
    - Use a stirrer or a spoon to mix the ingredients thoroughly.
4. Garnish:
    - Garnish the cocktail with a celery stalk or a pickled asparagus spear.
    - Optionally, add a lemon wedge or any other preferred garnish such as lime wedge, horseradish, or pickled beans.
5. Serve:
    - Serve the Canadian Club Caesar cocktail immediately and enjoy its refreshing and savory flavors.

Tips for Making Canadian Club Caesar Cocktail:

- Adjust Flavor: Feel free to adjust the amount of Clamato juice, hot sauce, or Worcestershire sauce to suit your taste preferences. Some people prefer a spicier Caesar with more hot sauce.

- Garnishes: The garnishes not only add visual appeal but also enhance the flavor profile of the cocktail. Experiment with different garnishes to find your favorite combination.
- Variations: You can customize the Caesar cocktail further by adding ingredients like pickle juice, horseradish, or even a splash of beer (creating a "Red Eye" variation).

The Canadian Club Caesar cocktail is a beloved drink in Canada, especially enjoyed during brunch or as a refreshing cocktail on a warm day. It's a great way to experience a unique blend of flavors that highlight Canadian whisky and the savory tang of Clamato juice.

Ontario Butter Tart Cake

Ingredients:

For the Cake:

- 1 cup all-purpose flour
- 1 teaspoon baking powder
- 1/4 teaspoon salt
- 1/2 cup unsalted butter, softened
- 3/4 cup granulated sugar
- 2 large eggs
- 1 teaspoon vanilla extract
- 1/4 cup milk

For the Butter Tart Filling:

- 1/2 cup unsalted butter, melted
- 1 cup packed brown sugar
- 2 large eggs
- 1 teaspoon vanilla extract
- 1/4 cup all-purpose flour
- 1/2 cup raisins or chopped pecans (optional)

Instructions:

1. Preheat the Oven and Prepare the Pan:
    - Preheat your oven to 350°F (175°C). Grease and flour a 9-inch round cake pan or line it with parchment paper for easy removal.
2. Make the Cake Batter:
    - In a medium bowl, whisk together the flour, baking powder, and salt.
    - In a separate large bowl, cream together the softened butter and sugar until light and fluffy.
    - Beat in the eggs, one at a time, until well combined. Stir in the vanilla extract.
    - Gradually add the dry ingredients to the wet ingredients, alternating with the milk, beginning and ending with the flour mixture. Mix until just combined.
3. Prepare the Butter Tart Filling:
    - In a bowl, whisk together the melted butter, brown sugar, eggs, vanilla extract, and flour until smooth.

        - Stir in the raisins or chopped pecans, if using.
    4. **Assemble the Cake:**
        - Pour the cake batter into the prepared cake pan, spreading it evenly.
        - Carefully pour the butter tart filling over the cake batter, spreading it gently to cover the surface evenly.
    5. **Bake the Cake:**
        - Bake in the preheated oven for 35-40 minutes, or until the top is golden brown and a toothpick inserted into the center comes out clean or with a few moist crumbs.
    6. **Cool and Serve:**
        - Allow the cake to cool in the pan for 10 minutes, then transfer it to a wire rack to cool completely.
        - Slice and serve the Ontario Butter Tart Cake at room temperature. Optionally, dust with powdered sugar before serving.

Tips for Ontario Butter Tart Cake:

- **Variations:** Feel free to customize the cake by adding ingredients like chopped nuts (pecans or walnuts), raisins, or even a drizzle of caramel sauce over the top before serving.
- **Storage:** Store leftover cake in an airtight container at room temperature for up to 3 days, or refrigerate for longer storage.
- **Serving Suggestions:** Enjoy the cake on its own or with a dollop of whipped cream or a scoop of vanilla ice cream for a decadent dessert experience.

Ontario Butter Tart Cake is a delightful twist on the classic butter tart, offering all the flavors in a moist and tender cake format. It's perfect for special occasions, afternoon tea, or whenever you crave a taste of Ontario's sweet culinary tradition.

Saskatchewan Lentil Soup

Ingredients:

- 1 cup dry lentils (green or brown), rinsed and drained
- 1 tablespoon olive oil
- 1 onion, chopped
- 2 carrots, peeled and diced
- 2 celery stalks, diced
- 3 cloves garlic, minced
- 1 teaspoon ground cumin
- 1 teaspoon ground coriander
- 1/2 teaspoon smoked paprika
- 1 bay leaf
- 6 cups vegetable or chicken broth
- 1 can (14 oz) diced tomatoes
- Salt and pepper, to taste
- Fresh parsley or cilantro, chopped (for garnish)
- Lemon wedges, for serving (optional)

Instructions:

1. Prepare Lentils:
    - Rinse the lentils under cold water until the water runs clear. Drain and set aside.
2. Saute Vegetables:
    - In a large pot or Dutch oven, heat the olive oil over medium heat.
    - Add the chopped onion, diced carrots, and celery. Cook for about 5-7 minutes, or until the vegetables start to soften.
    - Add the minced garlic, ground cumin, ground coriander, smoked paprika, and bay leaf. Cook for another 1-2 minutes until fragrant.
3. Simmer Soup:
    - Stir in the rinsed lentils, vegetable or chicken broth, and diced tomatoes (with their juices).
    - Bring the soup to a boil, then reduce the heat to low. Cover and simmer for about 25-30 minutes, or until the lentils and vegetables are tender.
4. Season and Serve:
    - Season the soup with salt and pepper to taste.
    - Remove the bay leaf from the soup.
5. Garnish and Serve:

- Ladle the Saskatchewan Lentil Soup into bowls.
- Garnish with chopped fresh parsley or cilantro.
- Serve hot with lemon wedges on the side for squeezing over the soup, if desired.

Tips for Saskatchewan Lentil Soup:

- Variations: You can add other vegetables like potatoes, spinach, or bell peppers to the soup according to your preference.
- Texture: For a thicker soup, you can blend a portion of the soup with an immersion blender or in batches in a regular blender, then stir it back into the pot.
- Storage: Store leftover soup in an airtight container in the refrigerator for up to 4-5 days or freeze for longer storage. Reheat gently on the stovetop or in the microwave before serving.

Saskatchewan Lentil Soup is not only delicious and comforting but also a nutritious meal that showcases the flavor and versatility of lentils. It's perfect for warming up on a chilly day and makes a wholesome addition to any mealtime.

Nunavut Caribou Stew

Ingredients:

- 1 lb caribou meat, cut into bite-sized cubes (substitute with beef if caribou is unavailable)
- 2 tablespoons vegetable oil
- 1 onion, chopped
- 2 carrots, peeled and diced
- 2 celery stalks, diced
- 2 potatoes, peeled and diced
- 4 cups beef or caribou broth (or water)
- 1 bay leaf
- 1 teaspoon dried thyme
- Salt and pepper, to taste
- 1 cup frozen or fresh peas
- Fresh parsley, chopped (for garnish, optional)

Instructions:

1. Prepare the Caribou (or Beef):
   - If using caribou meat, ensure it is trimmed and cut into bite-sized cubes. If substituting with beef, you can use stewing beef.
2. Brown the Meat:
   - Heat the vegetable oil in a large pot or Dutch oven over medium-high heat.
   - Add the caribou meat cubes and brown them on all sides. This helps to develop flavor. If using beef, brown it similarly.
3. Saute Vegetables:
   - Add the chopped onion, diced carrots, diced celery, and diced potatoes to the pot with the browned meat. Cook for about 5-7 minutes, stirring occasionally, until the vegetables start to soften.
4. Simmer the Stew:
   - Pour in the beef or caribou broth (or water) to cover the meat and vegetables. Add the bay leaf and dried thyme.
   - Season with salt and pepper to taste. Bring the stew to a boil.
   - Reduce the heat to low, cover the pot, and let the stew simmer for about 1.5 to 2 hours, or until the meat is tender and the vegetables are cooked through.
5. Add Peas:

- Stir in the frozen or fresh peas during the last 10 minutes of cooking. This adds a vibrant color and texture to the stew.
6. Serve:
    - Remove the bay leaf from the stew before serving.
    - Ladle the Nunavut Caribou Stew into bowls.
    - Garnish with chopped fresh parsley, if desired, before serving.

Tips for Making Nunavut Caribou Stew:

- Traditional Ingredients: If possible, use caribou meat for an authentic taste of Nunavut. However, beef can be a suitable substitute.
- Variations: Some recipes may include additional ingredients such as turnips, parsnips, or barley for added flavor and texture.
- Cultural Significance: Caribou stew holds cultural importance in Inuit cuisine, providing warmth and sustenance in the harsh Arctic climate. It's often served during celebrations and gatherings.

Nunavut Caribou Stew is a wholesome and hearty dish that not only satisfies hunger but also celebrates the rich cultural heritage of the Inuit people in Canada's northern territories. Enjoy this stew as a comforting meal on cold days or as a way to explore traditional Indigenous foods.

New Brunswick Chicken Fricot

Ingredients:

For the Chicken Broth:

- 1 whole chicken (about 3-4 lbs), cut into pieces
- 8 cups water
- 2 onions, peeled and halved
- 2 carrots, peeled and chopped
- 2 celery stalks, chopped
- 2 bay leaves
- Salt and pepper, to taste

For the Soup:

- 2 tablespoons butter
- 1 onion, finely chopped
- 2 cloves garlic, minced
- 3 potatoes, peeled and diced
- 2 carrots, peeled and diced
- 2 celery stalks, diced
- 1 teaspoon dried thyme
- Salt and pepper, to taste
- Chopped fresh parsley, for garnish

For the Dumplings:

- 1 cup all-purpose flour
- 1 teaspoon baking powder
- 1/2 teaspoon salt
- 1/2 cup milk
- 2 tablespoons chopped fresh parsley (optional)

Instructions:

1. Prepare the Chicken Broth:
    - In a large pot, combine the chicken pieces, water, halved onions, chopped carrots, chopped celery, bay leaves, salt, and pepper.
    - Bring to a boil over high heat, then reduce the heat to medium-low. Skim off any foam that rises to the surface.

- Simmer, partially covered, for about 1 hour, or until the chicken is cooked through and tender.
        - Remove the chicken pieces from the broth and set aside to cool slightly. Once cool enough to handle, shred or chop the chicken into bite-sized pieces. Discard the skin and bones.
        - Strain the broth through a fine-mesh sieve into a clean bowl or pot. Discard the solids and return the broth to the pot. You should have about 6-7 cups of broth.
2. Make the Soup:
    - In the same pot with the strained broth, melt the butter over medium heat.
    - Add the finely chopped onion and minced garlic. Cook for about 3-4 minutes, until the onion is softened and translucent.
    - Stir in the diced potatoes, diced carrots, diced celery, and dried thyme. Cook for another 5 minutes, stirring occasionally.
    - Pour in the reserved chicken broth. Bring to a boil, then reduce the heat to low. Cover and simmer for about 15-20 minutes, or until the vegetables are tender.
3. Prepare the Dumplings:
    - In a medium bowl, whisk together the flour, baking powder, and salt.
    - Stir in the milk and chopped parsley (if using) until a soft dough forms.
    - Drop spoonfuls of the dumpling dough into the simmering soup. Cover and cook for 10-12 minutes, or until the dumplings are cooked through and puffed up.
4. Finish the Soup:
    - Stir in the shredded or chopped chicken pieces.
    - Season the soup with salt and pepper to taste.
5. Serve:
    - Ladle the New Brunswick Chicken Fricot into bowls.
    - Garnish with chopped fresh parsley.
    - Serve hot and enjoy this comforting Acadian soup with crusty bread on the side.

Tips for Making New Brunswick Chicken Fricot:

- Broth: Homemade chicken broth adds rich flavor to the soup. You can use store-bought chicken broth as a shortcut, but homemade is preferred for depth of flavor.
- Dumplings: Be sure to cover the pot while the dumplings are cooking to ensure they cook evenly and puff up nicely.

- Variations: Some recipes may include additional vegetables like turnips or parsnips. Feel free to adjust the vegetables and seasonings according to your preference.

New Brunswick Chicken Fricot is a comforting and nourishing soup that highlights the hearty flavors of chicken and vegetables, perfect for warming up during cold weather or as a satisfying meal any time of the year.

Prince Edward Island Mussel Chowder

Ingredients:

- 2 lbs fresh mussels, cleaned and debearded
- 4 slices bacon, chopped
- 1 tablespoon butter
- 1 onion, chopped
- 2 cloves garlic, minced
- 2 celery stalks, diced
- 2 carrots, peeled and diced
- 2 potatoes, peeled and diced
- 1 bay leaf
- 1 teaspoon dried thyme
- 3 cups seafood or vegetable broth
- 1 cup milk or cream (or a combination)
- Salt and pepper, to taste
- Chopped fresh parsley, for garnish
- Crusty bread, for serving

Instructions:

1. Prepare the Mussels:
    - Scrub the mussels under cold water to remove any dirt or debris. Pull off the beards (the fibrous threads sticking out of the shells) and discard any mussels that are open and do not close when tapped.
    - Place the cleaned mussels in a bowl of cold water and set aside.
2. Cook the Bacon and Vegetables:
    - In a large pot or Dutch oven, cook the chopped bacon over medium heat until crisp. Remove the bacon with a slotted spoon and set aside on a plate lined with paper towels.
    - Drain off excess bacon fat, leaving about 1 tablespoon in the pot. Add the butter.
    - Add the chopped onion, minced garlic, diced celery, diced carrots, and diced potatoes to the pot. Cook for about 5-7 minutes, stirring occasionally, until the vegetables start to soften.
3. Simmer the Chowder:
    - Pour in the seafood or vegetable broth. Add the bay leaf and dried thyme.
    - Bring the mixture to a boil, then reduce the heat to low. Cover and simmer for about 15 minutes, or until the vegetables are tender.

4. Prepare the Mussels:
   - While the chowder is simmering, discard any mussels that have not opened after soaking.
   - Add the cleaned mussels to the pot with the simmering broth and vegetables.
   - Cover the pot and cook for about 5-7 minutes, or until all the mussels have opened. Discard any mussels that remain closed.
5. Finish the Chowder:
   - Remove the bay leaf from the chowder.
   - Stir in the cooked bacon pieces and pour in the milk or cream (or a combination). Heat through gently without boiling.
   - Season the chowder with salt and pepper to taste.
6. Serve:
   - Ladle the Prince Edward Island Mussel Chowder into bowls.
   - Garnish with chopped fresh parsley.
   - Serve hot with crusty bread on the side for dipping.

Tips for Making Prince Edward Island Mussel Chowder:

- Fresh Mussels: It's important to use fresh mussels for this recipe. Discard any mussels that do not open during cooking, as they may be unsafe to eat.
- Creaminess: Adjust the amount of milk or cream to achieve your desired level of creaminess in the chowder.
- Variations: Some recipes may include additional ingredients like corn, leeks, or bacon for added flavor and texture.

Prince Edward Island Mussel Chowder is a delightful way to enjoy the fresh seafood flavors of the region. It's perfect for seafood lovers and a comforting meal to enjoy year-round, especially during cooler months.

Yukon Bison Stew

Ingredients:

- 2 lbs bison stew meat, cut into bite-sized pieces
- 2 tablespoons vegetable oil
- Salt and pepper, to taste
- 1 onion, chopped
- 2 cloves garlic, minced
- 2 carrots, peeled and diced
- 2 celery stalks, diced
- 2 potatoes, peeled and diced
- 1 parsnip, peeled and diced
- 1 turnip, peeled and diced
- 1 bay leaf
- 1 teaspoon dried thyme
- 4 cups beef or bison broth
- 1 cup red wine (optional)
- 1 tablespoon Worcestershire sauce
- Chopped fresh parsley, for garnish

Instructions:

1. Brown the Bison Meat:
    - Heat the vegetable oil in a large pot or Dutch oven over medium-high heat.
    - Season the bison stew meat with salt and pepper.
    - Working in batches, brown the bison meat on all sides. Remove the browned meat to a plate and set aside.
2. Saute Vegetables:
    - In the same pot, add the chopped onion and garlic. Cook for about 3-4 minutes, until softened and fragrant.
    - Add the diced carrots, diced celery, diced potatoes, diced parsnip, and diced turnip to the pot. Cook for another 5 minutes, stirring occasionally.
3. Simmer the Stew:
    - Return the browned bison meat to the pot.
    - Add the bay leaf, dried thyme, beef or bison broth, red wine (if using), and Worcestershire sauce to the pot. Stir well to combine.
    - Bring the stew to a boil, then reduce the heat to low. Cover and simmer for about 1.5 to 2 hours, or until the bison meat is tender and the vegetables are cooked through.

4. Finish and Serve:
   - Remove the bay leaf from the stew.
   - Taste and adjust seasoning with salt and pepper, if needed.
5. Garnish and Serve:
   - Ladle the Yukon Bison Stew into bowls.
   - Garnish with chopped fresh parsley.
   - Serve hot and enjoy this hearty stew with crusty bread or alongside mashed potatoes.

Tips for Making Yukon Bison Stew:

- Bison Meat: Bison stew meat is leaner than beef, so take care not to overcook it to maintain tenderness.
- Red Wine: The red wine adds depth to the flavor of the stew, but you can omit it if desired or substitute with additional broth.
- Vegetables: Feel free to customize the vegetables according to what you have on hand or prefer. Other root vegetables like rutabaga or sweet potatoes can also be used.

Yukon Bison Stew is a comforting and nutritious dish that highlights the natural flavors of bison meat and Yukon-grown vegetables. It's perfect for colder days and a great way to experience the flavors of Yukon's local ingredients.

Northern Ontario Pickerel Fillets

Ingredients:

- 4 pickerel fillets, skin-on (about 6-8 oz each)
- Salt and pepper, to taste
- 2 tablespoons vegetable oil
- 2 tablespoons unsalted butter
- 2 cloves garlic, minced
- 1 tablespoon fresh lemon juice
- 1 tablespoon chopped fresh parsley, for garnish
- Lemon wedges, for serving

Instructions:

1. Prepare the Pickerel Fillets:
    - Pat the pickerel fillets dry with paper towels. Season both sides generously with salt and pepper.
2. Heat the Pan:
    - Heat the vegetable oil in a large skillet over medium-high heat until shimmering but not smoking.
3. Cook the Pickerel Fillets:
    - Carefully place the pickerel fillets in the hot skillet, skin-side down. Cook for about 4-5 minutes, or until the skin is golden and crispy.
    - Flip the fillets and cook for an additional 2-3 minutes, or until the fish is cooked through and flakes easily with a fork.
4. Add Butter and Garlic:
    - Reduce the heat to medium-low. Add the unsalted butter and minced garlic to the skillet. Allow the butter to melt and the garlic to become fragrant, stirring gently to coat the fish with the buttery mixture.
5. Finish and Serve:
    - Remove the skillet from the heat.
    - Drizzle the pickerel fillets with fresh lemon juice.
    - Garnish with chopped fresh parsley.
    - Serve the Northern Ontario Pickerel Fillets hot, with lemon wedges on the side for squeezing over the fish.

Tips for Cooking Pickerel Fillets:

- Freshness: Ensure the pickerel fillets are fresh for the best flavor and texture. Look for fillets that are firm and have a mild scent.
- Skin-on Fillets: Cooking the pickerel fillets skin-on helps to retain moisture and adds flavor. The skin becomes crispy when cooked properly.
- Variations: You can customize the seasoning by adding herbs like thyme or dill, or a sprinkle of paprika for a bit of spice.

Northern Ontario Pickerel Fillets are a delightful dish that highlights the natural flavors of freshwater fish. This recipe is quick and easy, perfect for a weeknight meal or to impress guests with the taste of Ontario's northern lakes. Enjoy this delicious fish with a side of vegetables or a light salad for a complete meal.

Ontario Cherry Clafoutis

Ingredients:

- 1 lb fresh cherries, pitted
- 3 large eggs
- 1/2 cup granulated sugar
- 1 cup whole milk
- 1/2 cup all-purpose flour
- 1 teaspoon vanilla extract
- Pinch of salt
- Powdered sugar, for dusting

Instructions:

1. Prepare the Cherries:
    - Preheat your oven to 350°F (175°C).
    - Wash and pit the cherries. You can leave the stems intact for presentation, if desired.
2. Make the Batter:
    - In a large bowl, whisk together the eggs and granulated sugar until pale and fluffy.
    - Gradually whisk in the milk, followed by the flour, vanilla extract, and a pinch of salt. Whisk until the batter is smooth and well combined.
3. Assemble and Bake:
    - Grease a 9-inch round baking dish (or a similar size) with butter or cooking spray.
    - Arrange the pitted cherries in a single layer on the bottom of the baking dish.
    - Pour the batter evenly over the cherries.
4. Bake the Clafoutis:
    - Bake in the preheated oven for 40-45 minutes, or until the clafoutis is puffed, set in the center, and golden brown around the edges.
5. Serve:
    - Remove the clafoutis from the oven and let it cool slightly.
    - Dust with powdered sugar just before serving.
    - Serve warm or at room temperature. Enjoy the Ontario Cherry Clafoutis on its own or with a dollop of whipped cream or vanilla ice cream.

Tips for Making Ontario Cherry Clafoutis:

- Cherry Varieties: You can use any variety of fresh cherries available, such as Bing cherries or Rainier cherries, depending on your preference.
- Pitting Cherries: Use a cherry pitter or a small paring knife to remove the pits from the cherries. Alternatively, you can leave the pits in for a more traditional presentation, but warn guests before serving.
- Batter Consistency: The batter should be smooth and pourable. If you prefer a thicker clafoutis, you can increase the amount of flour slightly.

Ontario Cherry Clafoutis is a simple yet elegant dessert that highlights the natural sweetness of fresh cherries. It's perfect for summer gatherings or any occasion when you want to enjoy a taste of Ontario's seasonal fruit.

Quebecois Pouding Chômeur (Poor Man's Pudding)

Ingredients:

For the Cake Batter:

- 1 cup all-purpose flour
- 2 teaspoons baking powder
- 1/4 teaspoon salt
- 1/2 cup granulated sugar
- 1/2 cup milk
- 2 tablespoons unsalted butter, melted

For the Sauce:

- 1 cup packed brown sugar
- 1 cup water
- 1/4 cup unsalted butter

Instructions:

1. Preheat the Oven:
    - Preheat your oven to 375°F (190°C). Grease an 8-inch square baking dish or a similar-sized baking dish with butter or cooking spray.
2. Make the Cake Batter:
    - In a mixing bowl, whisk together the flour, baking powder, salt, and granulated sugar.
    - Stir in the milk and melted butter until you have a smooth batter. The batter will be thick.
    - Spread the batter evenly into the prepared baking dish.
3. Prepare the Sauce:
    - In a saucepan, combine the brown sugar, water, and 1/4 cup of unsalted butter.
    - Bring the mixture to a boil over medium-high heat, stirring occasionally to dissolve the sugar and melt the butter.
4. Assemble and Bake:
    - Pour the hot sauce evenly over the cake batter in the baking dish. Do not stir.
    - Place the baking dish on a baking sheet (to catch any potential spills) and transfer to the preheated oven.

- Bake for 30-35 minutes, or until the top is golden brown and the cake is cooked through. The sauce will thicken as it bakes.
5. Serve:
    - Remove the Quebecois Pouding Chômeur from the oven and let it cool slightly.
    - Serve warm, spooning the cake and sauce into bowls.
    - Optional: Serve with a scoop of vanilla ice cream or a dollop of whipped cream for extra indulgence.

Tips for Making Quebecois Pouding Chômeur:

- Sauce Consistency: The sauce should be thick and syrupy when poured over the cake batter. It will continue to thicken as it bakes.
- Variations: Some recipes may include a hint of vanilla extract or maple syrup in the sauce for added flavor. Feel free to customize according to your taste preferences.
- Storage: Leftovers can be stored covered in the refrigerator for up to 3 days. Reheat gently in the microwave or oven before serving.

Quebecois Pouding Chômeur is a beloved dessert in Quebec, cherished for its simplicity and rich, comforting flavors. It's a wonderful way to enjoy a taste of French-Canadian culinary heritage and is sure to be a hit with family and friends.

Canadian Rocky Road Ice Cream

Ingredients:

- 2 cups heavy cream
- 1 cup whole milk
- 3/4 cup granulated sugar
- 4 large egg yolks
- 1 teaspoon vanilla extract
- 1/2 cup semi-sweet chocolate chips or chopped chocolate
- 1/2 cup mini marshmallows
- 1/2 cup chopped walnuts or pecans

Instructions:

1. Prepare the Ice Cream Base:
    - In a saucepan, combine the heavy cream, whole milk, and granulated sugar over medium heat. Stir occasionally until the mixture begins to steam and small bubbles form around the edges. Do not boil.
2. Temper the Egg Yolks:
    - In a separate bowl, whisk the egg yolks until smooth.
    - Gradually add about 1 cup of the hot cream mixture to the egg yolks, whisking constantly. This step tempers the eggs to prevent scrambling.
    - Pour the tempered egg mixture back into the saucepan with the remaining cream mixture, whisking constantly.
3. Cook the Custard:
    - Cook the mixture over medium-low heat, stirring constantly with a wooden spoon or heatproof spatula. Cook until the mixture thickens slightly and coats the back of the spoon, about 5-7 minutes. Do not let it boil.
    - Remove from heat and stir in the vanilla extract. Strain the custard through a fine-mesh sieve into a clean bowl to remove any cooked egg bits.
4. Chill the Custard:
    - Cover the custard with plastic wrap, pressing the wrap directly onto the surface to prevent a skin from forming.
    - Refrigerate the custard until completely chilled, at least 4 hours or overnight.
5. Churn the Ice Cream:
    - Once chilled, pour the custard into your ice cream maker and churn according to the manufacturer's instructions until it reaches a soft-serve consistency.

6. Add Mix-Ins:
    - During the last few minutes of churning, add the chocolate chips (or chopped chocolate), mini marshmallows, and chopped nuts. Churn just until evenly distributed.
7. Freeze the Ice Cream:
    - Transfer the churned ice cream into a freezer-safe container. Press a piece of parchment paper or plastic wrap directly onto the surface of the ice cream to prevent ice crystals from forming.
    - Freeze for at least 4 hours or until firm before serving.
8. Serve:
    - Scoop the Canadian Rocky Road Ice Cream into bowls or cones.
    - Enjoy the creamy, chocolatey, nutty goodness of this Canadian-inspired treat!

Tips for Making Canadian Rocky Road Ice Cream:

- Mix-Ins: Customize the ice cream by adding more or less of the mix-ins to suit your taste. You can also substitute walnuts or pecans with almonds or hazelnuts.
- Storage: Store any leftover ice cream in an airtight container in the freezer for up to a few weeks. Let it soften slightly at room temperature for a few minutes before scooping.
- Variations: For a Canadian twist, consider using maple syrup instead of vanilla extract in the custard for a hint of maple flavor.

This Canadian Rocky Road Ice Cream recipe is perfect for summer days or any time you crave a delicious frozen dessert. It combines the classic flavors of Rocky Road with the richness of homemade ice cream, making it a delightful treat for all ages.

www.ingramcontent.com/pod-product-compliance
Lightning Source LLC
LaVergne TN
LVHW081602060526
838201LV00054B/2028